# Tracy McGrady: The Inspiring Story of One of Basketball's Greatest Shooting Guards

## An Unauthorized Biography

## By: Clayton Geoffreys

# Table of Contents

# Foreword

Entering the new millennium, one of the fastest rising stars in the NBA was Tracy McGrady. After leaving the Toronto Raptors for the Orlando Magic, McGrady quickly blossomed into a superstar caliber player, wowing fans with his incredible ability to get to the basket and to score. Though he would often not have the necessary pieces around him to win a championship, he was a dominant shooting guard throughout the 2000s that forced opposing teams to warrant a double team.

In a later interview, Kobe Bryant would actually state that Tracy McGrady was one of the hardest players to match up against in his prime. It's no surprise why if you've ever looked up a series of highlights from Tracy McGrady's prime years.

Thank you for purchasing *Tracy McGrady: The Inspiring Story of One of Basketball's Greatest Shooting Guards*. In this unauthorized biography, we will learn Tracy McGrady's incredible life story and impact on the game of basketball. Hope you enjoy and if you do, please do not forget to leave a review!

Also, check out my website at claytongeoffreys.com to join my exclusive list where I let you know about my latest books. To thank you for your purchase, you can go to my site to download a free copy of *33 Life Lessons: Success Principles, Career Advice & Habits of Successful People*. In the book, you'll learn from some of the greatest thought leaders of different industries on what it takes to become successful and how to live a great life.

Cheers,

*Clayton Geoffreys*

*Visit me at www.claytongeoffreys.com*

# Introduction

Can there be such a thing in basketball as too much talent? Outside of the basketball court, we frequently talk about those who get too talented, too quickly. Some people grow up to be natural geniuses. However, these geniuses tend to coast on their talents and never become diligent or mature enough to fulfill their potential. Sometimes, they get surpassed by those of lesser talent, those who have learned to work even harder thanks to their lack of talent.

"Hard work beats talent when talent does not work hard." That's a saying that applies to today's reality. No matter how much talent you have, hard workers will always trump your talent whenever you do not work half as hard as they do. In that regard, the best players we have seen in the history of the game tend to be the ones that worked the hardest.

Michael Jordan, for all the different things that he did on the side, worked his tail off to become the greatest player of his generation. Kobe Bryant looked at Jordan and used what he learned to become the closest player to MJ we have ever seen in the history of the sport. Meanwhile, LeBron James ended up working hard on his body and conditioning to be able to play more than two decades of high-level basketball. And Stephen Curry became the greatest shooter in the history of the game because he worked hard on honing his craft.

So, when it comes to the best players we've seen in the NBA, there is usually a combination of talent and hard work. There have been those who were given great talent, and they worked harder than anyone else to hone those talents. Kevin Durant was born to become nearly seven feet tall but he never rested on his laurels. Instead, he used his physical tools to become an unguardable scorer. The same can be said about Giannis Antetokounmpo, who uses his raw physical gifts to become unstoppable whenever he attacks the basket.

That is why, in many ways, a player needs to be very talented for him to become one of the greatest players of his generation. Some of these players were born with incredible physical abilities and skills that allowed them to stand out and become better than anyone else. And one such player was Tracy McGrady, who ended up becoming one of the most popular players of his generation because of his incredible scoring talents.

When we look at Tracy McGrady, you could argue that he was the most talented shooting guard ever—maybe even above Jordan and Kobe. There was simply nothing McGrady could not do. He was a bigger wingman than any other superstar shooting guard in history. He was just as athletic as any other great off-guard the league has ever had. Plus, T-Mac had the skills that could rival those of Mike and Bryant. While McGrady's high school career made it look like he could become a great college player, the potential that he showed at a single basketball camp was so immense that he went straight from high school to an NBA lottery pick.

After several seasons as a role player, McGrady eventually developed into one of the premier superstars in the NBA and led his teams to regular season wins and the playoffs season after season. But while McGrady was blessed with more natural talent than almost all NBA players, he was cursed to have some of the worst teammates for any NBA superstar.

When he played for the Toronto Raptors in the early part of his career, he was a teenager playing alongside Marcus Camby, Doug Christie, Damon Stoudamire, and his cousin Vince Carter. At that point, he was seldom used and was merely a role player who was trying to get his huge break as a star.

When he played in Orlando, he was paired with the often-injured Grant Hill. It was only when he moved to Houston that he was able to play for a good playoff team, as he was teamed up with the 7'6" Chinese center, Yao Ming. However, injuries to him and Yao hindered the Rockets from playing their best.

Despite McGrady's impressive numbers over the years, his defining legacy was his inability to get past the first round of the NBA Playoffs. For years, he struggled on teams whose other stars were injured and lacked the role players to make up for it. Unfortunately, when it appeared that he would be on a championship squad in 2008-09, his body broke down from years of carrying poor teams. At that point in his life, he was merely entering his 30s. At that age, most NBA superstars were still in the prime years of their careers.

But McGrady was a different case. His body had been bearing the wear and tear of playing as a one-man superstar for most of his NBA career. His athletic abilities were all but gone by then. Perhaps we could use the example of Tracy McGrady as an example of the limitations of talent. It's possible that if McGrady had worked harder, he could have taken better care of his body and avoided the injuries that ultimately finished his career.

You look at guys like Michael Jordan and Kobe Bryant, who are two of the greatest shooting guards to ever play the game. Both players used their athletic ability to get thousands of points early in their careers. As time went on, they lost a lot of their hops and quickness. They had to rely on their fundamental skills, despite the wear and tear of injuries and the decay of time. Even when they reached their deep 30s, both shooting guards played at the highest level possible. McGrady could have been included in the conversation of best shooting guards had he worked as hard as Mike and Kobe did. He could have probably been the best, given his natural size and talent.

On the other hand, one could use Tracy McGrady as an example of the importance of luck in basketball. If McGrady had joined the Lakers, with Shaq and Kobe Bryant stuck in Orlando with Mike Miller and a perennially injured Grant Hill, how different would our memories be of those two players?

If he had been drafted by the Spurs in 1997, he could have played for one of the best organizations and one of the greatest coaches in NBA history. If he could have signed with the Detroit Pistons in the early 2000s, he could have been part of the best defensive team in the era. While it would be a step too far to call Tracy McGrady's career "tragic," it seems that when we look back, we do not remember McGrady's greatness as much as his failings. However, we should bear in mind that whatever his faults, McGrady is one of the greatest shooting guards in the history of the NBA, especially during his prime years.

There were not a lot of players who could compare to him as a scorer during his prime. Even the late great Kobe Bryant once admitted that T-Mac was the toughest player he ever had to guard during his younger years. Bryant had seen his fair share of great scorers, but McGrady had every move in his arsenal to make life difficult for Kobe, who was incredibly talented as a defender. In that regard, the talent was there for him. It was just that things did not go as planned for McGrady when it came to the trajectory of his career.

As such, McGrady ended his career not being able to win a championship or even play at the highest level possible during the latter stages of his career. He became a great "what-if" story to a lot of fans of the game. But the one thing that could never be taken away from him was his immense talent. It was his talent that turned him into a phenom that kids who grew up during the early 2000s love seeing. That is why T-Mac was one of the greatest scoring talents the world of basketball has ever seen. And the only way for anyone to appreciate just how good he was in his prime is to examine his life and how he got to the point wherein some fans thought that he was the best individual player in the league.

# Chapter 1: Childhood and Early Life

Tracy Lamar McGrady Jr. was born on May 24, 1979. He was raised almost entirely by his mother Melanise Williford, who carried Tracy when she was merely a teenager. He grew up with his mother in Bartow, Florida, which is a small city located in the central part of the state. Tracy Sr. got in touch with his son now and then, but Tracy Jr. has stated that he thought little of his father even then.[i]

Shortly after Tracy's birth, Melanise moved north to Auburndale, Florida, to live with her mother, Roberta. Auburndale is located about 40 minutes away from Orlando. It is a small, primarily white town of fewer than 15,000 people. While it was never an entirely safe neighborhood, Tracy and his little brother Chance roamed the streets of the city without incident. The nickname "T-Mac" did not exist then; instead, everyone called him "Pumpkin Head" or "Baked Beans," after his favorite foods.[ii] Tracy's family was not wealthy, but his mother and grandmother worked to provide a good life for him and gave him spending money on his birthday. McGrady got along well with both of them and called his grandmother "mom."

McGrady grew up as a natural athlete and played sports, but it was baseball, not basketball, which he loved as a child. He was an excellent pitcher and hitter and was a Little League star. Like Babe Ruth, he would point to exactly where he intended to hit the ball and do so. McGrady also learned to throw the knuckleball by the time he was 13 years old. He preferred pitching to hitting and idolized MLB pitcher Dwight Gooden.

"When I was younger, I started baseball at 5. That was my favorite sport. Even in my NBA career, it is still my favorite sport. I played football when I was 8 years old. I didn't really start playing basketball until I was like 9, 10 years old. It was because I got bullied. I got older cousins, a neighborhood full of guys that were older. We used to go to the park all the time. I used to just stand around and watch. Didn't want to play, again, because it wasn't my sport," McGrady said.[iii]

But while McGrady really did love baseball, the problem was that he did not have the innate talent to excel at it. He did not immediately showcase his talents as a baseball player and was bullied by the other kids because he was not exactly good at it. The fact that he was bullied was actually important to his development as an athlete because he learned to use this as a way to become better. He started working more on his baseball skills until he was good enough to compete with the other kids.

As much as McGrady loved baseball, basketball inevitably found him. By the age of 12, McGrady was already six feet tall. His height meant that local coaches and peers inquired about his interest in basketball. Also, the Orlando Magic had just joined the NBA as an expansion team and quickly achieved NBA success behind Shaquille O'Neal and star guard Penny Hardaway.

As nobody was as gifted in size as Shaq was, the young Tracy deeply idolized Penny as a basketball star. Hardaway was a 6'7" man but had the skills of a point guard on the floor. Tracy wanted to be like that because, at his age, he was already a tall boy. The Auburndale locals became more interested in basketball thanks to nearby Orlando's success, and McGrady grew up wanting to play just like Penny Hardaway.[iv]

Back then, as a young boy, McGrady liked playing basketball. But it was more of a one-on-one style that he loved. Kids did not always play organized basketball on the playgrounds. Because Tracy was exposed to the sport watching other kids playing it, he was not familiar with the way that organized basketball was supposed to be played. As such, he preferred playing one-on-one with the other kids in his neighborhood.

"That introduced me to one-on-one basketball from that point on. As I got older, that's all I did was play one-on-one. That became getting tough and being able to figure out defenses and how they play. Playing through bigger and stronger guys, quicker guys, that was my niche," McGrady said.[ii]

Of course, playing one-on-one with the neighbors allowed McGrady to learn some of the few tricks of the trade. He saw just how difficult it was to play against bigger kids at that time. This allowed him to learn how to toughen up as a player and discover new tricks that would allow him to score against kids who were older than he was.

And it was by playing one-on-one that T-Mac eventually became an unstoppable isolation player who could break his man down off the dribble and score over any kind of defense that he saw.

The unorthodox setup that he experienced when he was still just a kid helped him learn how to defeat his opponents all on his own without having to rely on a team setup. While a team setup would always be much more important for a player to learn how to play within a team, it was McGrady's experiences when he was still just a boy that honed his athletic talents. And as he grew older, he found out that basketball was his calling.

Of course, he still loved baseball more than basketball. The sport of basketball was a fun activity for him to do with his friends, especially when he wanted to play one-on-one with the other kids in the neighborhood. But baseball was the sport that he really wanted to excel at when he was a young boy. That was why it took a while for him to realize that he was a better basketball player than a baseball player. And this sounds eerily similar to Michael Jordan's path as a basketball superstar because we know that MJ loved playing baseball as a young boy and was even urged by his father to choose it over basketball.

Of course, the McGrady and Jordan comparisons were yet to exist at that time. That was because McGrady was yet to completely fall in love with basketball. On the other hand, Jordan was already dominating the NBA during T-Mac's formative years as a young boy.

And it did not take long for him to become one of the players who fans thought could take the baton from Jordan and carry it into the future.

# Chapter 2: High School Years

Despite Tracy McGrady's growing interest in basketball, baseball remained his primary passion in his first two years at Auburndale High School. At the time, Tracy was not a particularly distinguished athlete in either sport. He made the varsity basketball team as a freshman but received little playing time. In that regard, he did not even think about playing basketball as a career. He was good at the sport but he never thought that he was going to become one of the greatest players in the era. As such, McGrady's primary focus continued to be the sport of baseball.

Not much changed in his second year of high school. He still was not a star at that point in his life. McGrady did not have the size or skills to become one of the best players in his age group. While he was athletic, he was not athletic enough to stand out as a high school basketball player while there were bigger and more experienced teenagers that were given more playing time. Even so, he was already being used as a role player, as he showed some improvements from his freshman year. His skills were evolving. It was just that he did not yet have the size or athletic abilities that would enable him to keep up with his growing set of skills in the sport.

But things began to change for Tracy McGrady during his junior year. He grew from 6'3'' to 6'8'', which practically forced him out of baseball and into basketball. This was the growth spurt that he was waiting for because the extra five inches that he got made him a much better player. And the thing was that he had guard skills even before his growth spurt because he played more like a guard at his shorter height before he became 6'8".

In many cases, the height of a player determines his playing position. This was almost always the case in the United States, where players are often trained to hone skills at their respective positions from the very beginning of their careers. That was why McGrady worked on guard skills before his growth spurt—because a player standing 6'3" was almost guaranteed to play the role of a guard his entire life.

There was also the fact that he played one-on-one a lot in the playground. Those who have experienced playing one-on-one would understand how important this is in developing the guard skills of a player. And because T-Mac idolized Penny Hardaway, he wanted to develop the same guard skills that his favorite player had.

Coach Ty Willis also began to use him more.[v] After averaging 16 points per game as a sophomore, McGrady had an outstanding junior year and averaged 26 points and 12 rebounds. He had become a clear threat at the high school level because he had incredible guard skills at his new height. The growth spurt allowed him to retain his skills and mobility while also making him as tall as a smaller power forward. Tracy grew into his athleticism and started outjumping most of his peers.

There was also the fact that he worked hard to become the best player that he could become. Now that he understood that basketball was his calling because of his massive growth spurt, McGrady worked hard to improve his basketball skills and routinely showed up at the court at 5:30 a.m. to practice for the next three to four hours. It wasn't long before college recruiters across the country took notice and began to consider offering McGrady a scholarship. And that was when it became clear that he could be one of the most sought-after young prospects in the entire country.

However, McGrady nearly threw his chances away thanks to his off-court behavior. While he was a hard worker on the court, Tracy routinely skipped classes and argued with teachers. He was never a student who consistently did well in class or even showed up in the first place. When he did indeed come to class, his mind was wandering elsewhere since he focused more on basketball.

Because of that, his grades slipped, so much so that McGrady was eventually kicked off the basketball team despite his prodigious talent. The potential scholarship offers were retracted as well. At the beginning of the summer of 1996, few people outside of Auburndale had heard of McGrady—and he had just one more highly uncertain year of high school left.

Still, McGrady had allies who were there to support him. His mother and grandmother urged him not to give up, and McGrady continued to work on basketball even though he had no idea if a college scholarship was going to come. McGrady also had the support of Alvis Smith, his Amateur Athletic Union (AAU) coach and a scout for Adidas. With his connections, Smith secured McGrady an invitation to the Adidas ABCD Camp in Teaneck, New Jersey.

The Adidas ABCD Camp is one of the most prestigious basketball camps for young men across the country. McGrady showed up at the camp with $25 in his pocket and the knowledge that if he wanted a future in basketball, he needed to submit an incredible performance. And that was exactly what he did.

McGrady's performance was not just amazing—it became one of the greatest summer camp performances in all of basketball history. Against other highly touted prospects like Ron Artest, Quentin Richardson, and above all, Lamar Odom, McGrady dominated the competition with his scoring and passing ability.

The highlight of McGrady's performance came when he faced off against highly touted New York prospect big man James Felton. McGrady drove past Felton and stunned him with a jaw-dropping windmill dunk the likes of which no one had ever seen. The game temporarily halted as spectators and fans went nuts. Odom called the dunk "one of the best basketball moments of my life." McGrady himself described it as the moment "which I knew I had arrived."

By the end of that camp, everyone knew who Tracy McGrady was. He had suddenly gone from an unknown to one of the biggest high school prospects in the country. However, McGrady still faced the problem of where he was going to play basketball next season. Would he be allowed back on the Auburndale High School team after getting kicked out?

But after the camp, Joel Hopkins, the coach of Mount Zion Christian Academy in Durham, North Carolina, showed up at McGrady's house. Hopkins offered Tracy the chance to play for Mount Zion but was upfront about what he would demand from the young man. McGrady would undergo a strict Christian education. He would run seven miles every morning before school began, would not be allowed to curse, date, or listen to rap music, and he would live with twelve other men in a house. He told Melanise that this was the best way for him to build character and become a better basketball player.

McGrady and his mother agreed to Hopkins's terms, and he departed for North Carolina shortly afterward. Any faint hopes of playing baseball were dashed by the fact that Mount Zion did not even have a baseball team. But under Coach Hopkins's strict discipline, McGrady's basketball skills continued to improve. He consistently made USA Today's list of the top 25 prospects in the nation and climbed the rankings as the season continued. McGrady did clash with Hopkins now and then, but he put up terrific numbers and led Mount Zion to success.

Mount Zion played one of the most challenging high school schedules in the country during the 1996-97 season, but they still finished with a 26-2 record. McGrady averaged 28 points, 7 rebounds, 6 assists, and 3 steals in his senior year of high school.

Tracy played all five positions whenever Hopkins required it, and was a terror on the defensive end as well. He was nominated the High School Player of the Year by *USA Today* and was also named a McDonald's All-American.

Off the court, McGrady even worked on his studies and managed to do well enough on the SAT to ensure that he could get into college. In contrast to the end of his junior year, colleges across the country flocked for the chance to sign him.

McGrady considered returning to Florida to play for Florida State, but Kentucky quickly took the lead in the recruitment process. McGrady was a fan of Kentucky and was intrigued by the chance to play for legendary coach Rick Pitino.

"I took my visit to a couple of colleges but I went to Kentucky and I saw how those boys was living, I said, 'This is where I want to go to school.' I was already a fan before I went there," McGrady said. "When I took that visit bro and I see how they were living up there as college athletes. I want to go to Kentucky."[vi]

Shockingly enough, when McGrady was about to commit to the Kentucky Wildcats, major NBA scout Marty Blake told Alvis Smith that if McGrady joined the 1997 NBA Draft, he would likely be selected in the first round, if not the lottery.

Potential superstar Tim Duncan would certainly be the first pick in the 1997 Draft, and Keith Van Horn would probably be taken next.

However, no one else was projected to be a surefire star or impact player within that draft class.[vii] Under those circumstances, NBA teams could be persuaded to select a young prospect with as much potential as McGrady.

Also, NBA teams were now warming up to selecting players directly out of high school. High school big man Kevin Garnett had been chosen with the 5th pick in 1995, and high school guard Kobe Bryant had also been taken in the first round of the 1996 Draft.

The thing about going directly from high school to the NBA was that it was going to help a player earn money quickly and get exposed to professional players who could mentor them at an earlier age. Getting exposed to the life of a professional NBA player would also help the player become more mature more quickly, especially because he would need to learn how to act like a mature adult while playing together and against grown men. But taking this leap was still a riskier proposition for a young prospect. The problem was, not all players who go straight from high school to the NBA get to find immediate success.

That is because high school players need to adjust to an entirely different life compared to what they experienced before going to the NBA. High school basketball is entirely different compared to the NBA because the player needs to adjust to 82 games a season while working non-stop during practices. And prep-to-pro players need to earn their spot on a roster because adults who went through college are never going to willingly allow a teenage upstart to take their spot and minutes.

That was why Kevin Garnett, for all his talents, did not start out well in the NBA. He was clearly incredibly talented when he got there. But the issue was that his mind and body still needed to adapt to the grind. Meanwhile, Kobe Bryant needed to find his place with the Lakers after getting drafted at the age of 17. His head coach did not want to give him more minutes because there were other players whom he thought were more deserving of minutes than an 18-year-old teenager who needed to earn the respect of the veterans on the team.

In that regard, getting to the NBA from the prep ranks was not always ideal for someone who had the same elite level of talent that Tracy McGrady had. He was already dominating the high school ranks and was undoubtedly ready for the NBA because he had the body and raw skills of a professional player. Nevertheless, going to college would have helped him develop more in terms of his mindset and skills. In fact, in hindsight, T-Mac once said that he thought players needed to go through at least two years of college before going to the NBA.

"I actually think they should implement having these guys go to school for two years," McGrady said. "What is it, one year now? At least go to school for two years because the league is so young. I think we need to build our league up."[viii]

McGrady attributed this evolved mindset to the fact that he struggled to get the minutes and touches that he wanted when he first got to the

NBA. Of course, that was because he needed to compete with and against grown men. That was one of the growing pains that he had to go through during his early NBA life.

"It was pretty difficult becoming a man so early and competing against grown men," McGrady said. "You're the best player on the floor in high school and then you come face the best players in the world. Also, the transition to living on your own, having to deal with the traveling, dealing with the different climates, getting into cities at 2 or 3 in the morning and then waking up the next morning for shootarounds and practices. I mean, it was a culture shock."[iv]

Nevertheless, McGrady had a choice to make during his senior year in high school. He liked the idea of going to the pros straight from the prep ranks. Smith told McGrady and Hopkins what he had heard, and the two adults concluded that the best move for McGrady would be to join the NBA. McGrady eventually agreed. In 1997, he announced his decision to enter the draft.

"I considered college, but my dream is to make it to the top," McGrady said. "And I had a chance to do that earlier."

He also said that he didn't join the draft because he was already prepared to play in the NBA. McGrady joined it because he wanted to, and because he could already play with the big boys in the NBA. True enough, he had the talent and skills to play against grown men in the professional ranks. He was bigger than most wings and was incredibly skilled for a young player who did not even take up basketball

22

seriously before his junior year. And he had the confidence that made him believe that he could get to the NBA and make a huge splash there.

Plus, at that point, Tracy was already signed with agent Arn Tellem. The NCAA, at that time, forbade players to sign with agents. Because of that, it was already too late for McGrady to retract his decision to go to the NBA instead of attending college. The fact was, he was already a phenom at that young age. His reputation had preceded him, and the hype was growing exponentially.

Tracy McGrady was not even in the NBA yet, but he already owned a Lexus. Major sports shoe companies Nike and Adidas were also quick to scout him as the next big thing in basketball. T-Mac would eventually sign with Adidas for a sum of $12 million for a span of six years. Keep in mind that he was still a high school player at that time and wasn't even drafted yet.

"I was able to judge very early. I wanted him to sign with Adidas," said Sonny Vaccaro, director of basketball for the company. "You've got to make sure you've got a pretty damn good person and it's tough to judge with a teenager." But after six months of observing McGrady on and off the court, Vaccaro concluded, "Let's roll the dice with this kid."[vii]

One of the reasons why he had already earned multiple deals at the age of 18 was the fact that the world was obsessed with young athletes who could very well be the next face of the sport of basketball.

Michael Jordan was already getting older at that time, but MJ was the biggest draw in the world of professional sports. He basically turned Nike into a sporting apparel empire after he joined the company in 1984 when it was still struggling to compete against bigger brands. So, when different companies learned that there was a 6'8" wing who had guard skills and the potential to become the next face of the sport, they were quick to jump on him even though he was not even in the NBA yet.

Some people might be quick to say that McGrady should have gone to college first. But judging his choice to join the NBA as a bad move was premature. Tracy was clearly inspired by how Garnett, Bryant, and Jermaine O'Neal had made the jump to the NBA from high school. And at that age, it is pretty easy to get caught up in your own hype, not to mention be tempted by all the lucrative aspects of turning pro.

Still, you cannot help but feel that he needed to mature first before going pro. Tracy had just shunned big NCAA basketball programs such as Kentucky and Florida State because he felt like he already had the skills to run with the big boys of the big league. Just a year prior, he was not even in the top 500 of the best college prospects. Even the best scouts of high school talents did not know who Tracy was. But, in 1997, he was a confident and cocky kid who had all the basketball gifts that a player of his size needed. He even went as far as describing himself as a combination of Scottie Pippen and Penny Hardaway. That may have been true at the prep level, but in the NBA, that was yet to be seen.

# Chapter 3: NBA Career

## Getting Drafted

As Tracy McGrady put it himself, he was a combination of Scottie Pippen and Penny Hardaway. Well, from a physical standpoint, he was not wrong. Tracy came into the NBA Draft measuring almost 6'8" and weighing a good 210 pounds. At that height and weight, McGrady was similar to Pippen as far as his physical stats. But what made McGrady even more like Pippen and Hardaway was his long arms.

Tracy's wingspan measured a whopping 7'2". While being tall and having long arms is a good thing, T-Mac was also a great athlete with a vertical leap of 40 inches. From those physical attributes alone, he was not wrong in comparing himself to Scottie and Penny.

Curtis Hill, an NBA scout, would point out that McGrady was a teenager of supreme athleticism.[ix] At his size, he could jump out of the building as good as guys who were shorter and smaller than he was. Furthermore, McGrady was also a gracefully quick athlete on the floor and could move just as smoothly and as fast as point and shooting guards. Another scout named Shivaram Shanmugam would even say that Tracy was an even better athlete than his cousin Vince Carter, whose best asset was his hops. With his long strides, speed, and incredible jumping abilities, McGrady was the greatest high school athlete in Florida when finishing in transition.

Offensively, Hill pointed out that McGrady's athleticism was his best asset when finishing at the basket. Not only was he able to jump higher than the defenders, he was able to contort his body mid-air to finish around the rim. As good an athlete as McGrady was, he did not rely on his physical attributes alone when it came to scoring. His jump shot, though not the best asset of his game, was a promising skill as he could shoot from anywhere on the floor and against any defense.

Despite his 6'8" frame, Tracy McGrady's ball handling was one of his biggest assets. Though he was not the best ball handler in high school, he was still better than most people his size. Idolizing Penny Hardaway, a 6'7" point guard, might have helped him develop those dribbling abilities when he was still younger. With his ball handling together with his finishing ability and shooting skills, Tracy McGrady was a supreme offensive talent even for a high school prospect.

As good as McGrady was as a potential future star in the NBA, he still had some downsides. Both Hill and Shanmugam pointed out that he was a stationary offensive player.[ix] When the ball was not in his hands, he barely moved on the floor. He did not have the habit of cutting to the basket or even running through screens. He was simply a player who relied on isolation plays and transition moments to score baskets. When the ball was not in Tracy's hands, you could expect him not to score except when he managed to get an offensive rebound.

McGrady also did not show a lot of skills on the defensive end of the floor. With his size, athleticism, and wingspan, Tracy had a lot of potential to be an excellent perimeter defender on the NBA level. However, with the level of competition he had in high school and with his advanced size for a teenager, McGrady did not have many opportunities to improve on that aspect of the game. He would simply block shots left and right when defending players one-on-one. But, in the NBA, players are bigger, longer, and more athletic than Tracy's high school competition. Just blocking shots would not do for a perimeter player. He would have to practice his skills in defending the perimeter.

Rebounding also was not a prime skill of Tracy McGrady's. Do not be fooled by his double-digit rebounding stats in high school. He was simply great at the boards because of his size and athleticism. But, when it came to fundamental rebounding skills such as boxing out, McGrady seemed like a slacker. His habit of moving without the ball also hurt his chances of getting offensive rebounds, as he would mostly dwell out on the perimeter.

Despite his shortcomings, McGrady still had a lot of superstar potential, as Isiah Thomas, a Toronto Raptor official at that time, would point out. All that Tracy needed was a little time to mature and a lot of experience to improve on the other aspects of his game. And the biggest reason why he was such an intriguing prospect was the fact that the NBA had become obsessed with players who were similar to Michael Jordan.

The league understood that Jordan's years of domination would not last forever. He was already 34 years old at that time, despite the fact that he was still the league's best player. But the NBA and the other organizations working closely with the league were seemingly constantly hunting for the heir to His Airness because the sport of basketball's value skyrocketed with Jordan's popularity. Also, no one could deny the fact that most kids who were getting drafted at that time grew up watching Air Jordan dominating the league.

So, in a sense, T-Mac was an intriguing prospect because he had all the tools to become the next great wing in the NBA. The league wanted a wing player to become the face of the NBA because these players attracted more attention than big men. True enough, there were still great big men in the league at that time, as Shaquille O'Neal was set to take over as the next big thing in the league. But centers did not command the same kind of attention from kids and teenagers that guards and wings did. That was why it made more sense for the league to look at guards and wings as future prospects who could become popular enough to turn into the next Jordan. And the league had already seen an influx of such players in the past few years, with the likes of Grand Hill, Penny Hardaway, Allen Iverson, and Kobe Bryant entering the league.

As the 1997 NBA Draft commenced, Tim Duncan, to nobody's surprise, was chosen first. He was followed by Keith Van Horn and Chauncey Billups. Billups and Antonio Daniels were the only guards chosen ahead of McGrady. When it was the Toronto Raptor's turn to choose a guy with their 9th overall pick, Thomas was surprised that McGrady was still available. The Raptors could have chosen Olivier Saint-Jean, a French player, with that pick. But they wanted Tracy instead because he had shown a lot of superstar potential.

McGrady had now become one of the newest members of the prep-to-pro club in the NBA. Of course, he eventually learned that high school players did not have it so easy in the NBA because they still needed to find their place and adjust to an entirely different level of competition. And in hindsight, he even said that spending at least a year in college would have better prepared him for the NBA.

Nevertheless, he never regretted his swift ascent to the NBA because this was the path that he had chosen for himself. He was now an NBA player just two years after he broke out of the scene as a junior in high school. T-Mac eventually learned the hard way that nothing was going to be given to him just because he was one of the best high school players in the entire country. The NBA was an entirely different monster that he needed to learn how to deal with.

## Rookie Season

In the early 1990s, the NBA expanded to cities across the United States and Canada. One of those new teams was the Toronto Raptors, which formed in 1995. Like most expansion teams, the Raptors got off to a slow start, winning just 51 games in total over their first two seasons. Despite the early struggles, many believed that general manager and NBA legend Isiah Thomas had assembled a potential championship core.

In 1995, the Raptors selected point guard Damon Stoudamire with the 7th pick, who would go on to win Rookie of the Year that season. Then the Raptors selected Marcus Camby in 1996 with the 2nd pick, and now McGrady in 1997. Ideally, Stoudamire, Camby, and McGrady would form a dynamic trio that would develop to bring a championship to Toronto. Isiah Thomas, the savvy former NBA player, would get the role players they would need to win.

In just a few short months, the dream crashed and burned. Isiah clashed with the Raptors ownership and left to announce for NBC. Damon Stoudamire was outraged by Thomas's departure, demanded a trade, and in February was sent to the Portland Trail Blazers for essentially nothing. Camby missed 20 games with an injury and offensively regressed from his rookie season. He would be traded that offseason for veteran Charles Oakley. Coach Darrell Walker lost the respect of the locker room and was fired after 49 games. The 1996-97 season was a total disaster for the Raptors. After winning 30 games in 1996-97, they lost 17 straight and won just 16 during the 1997-98 season.

The young Tracy McGrady was not immune to Toronto's mess. He was placed in trade rumors to the Philadelphia 76ers, failed to establish good relations with his teammates, and did not get along with Darrell Walker. Walker criticized McGrady's work ethic and was highly inconsistent with the young player's minutes.

For example, McGrady's first start was on December 31, 1997, against the Washington Wizards. He played for 30 minutes and scored 13 points. Walker played McGrady for just 18 minutes in the next game, and then just one minute in the next. For all these reasons, McGrady's first few months in the NBA were miserable. When he was in Toronto, he spent most of his days in his apartment watching videos.

Nevertheless, he still had good moments as a rookie player with a lot of star potential in him. On November 11th, McGrady had his first double-double game. He had 10 points and 11 rebounds in 23 minutes in a 28-point loss to the Indiana Pacers. T-Mac had seven huge offensive rebounds in that match. He then had 17 points and 7 rebounds (including 5 on the offensive end) against the Boston Celtics. He played 26 minutes while shooting 7 out of 11 from the field in that loss. Despite a few games here and there, McGrady was still mainly a bench player that could only get great moments when the game was unwinnable or when the Raptors had already been blown out early.

McGrady's fortunes improved when Walker was replaced by Coach Butch Carter. Carter told McGrady that he needed to improve his work ethic, but promised him that he would play him more if he did. McGrady listened to Carter's advice, and Carter began to give McGrady more playing time and consistent minutes.

On February 13th, McGrady scored above 20 points for the first time in his career. In that loss to the New Jersey Nets, he had 22 points and 8 rebounds in 37 minutes of action. He made 7 out of 16 shots from the field in that game. That performance was off a 14-point outing in a loss to the Cleveland Cavaliers.

After that season breakout, Tracy would score 17 points in another loss to the Miami Heat. He had 8 rebounds in 32 minutes that game while also shooting 7 out of 12 from the field. He would score 14 points together with 5 rebounds, 4 assists, and a then career-high 4 steals in the next game against Michael Jordan and Scottie Pippen of the Chicago Bulls. That was the end game of his best four-game stretch in his rookie season. Despite McGrady's good performances, the Toronto Raptors were deeply struggling as a team and franchise.

Early in April, when the season was all but a bust for the Toronto Raptors, the teenage Tracy McGrady was inserted into the starting lineup. He would also play starter's minutes. As a starter, he had two different streaks of scoring in double-digits in three straight games. First, he had 11 points and 9 boards in a loss to the Atlanta Hawks. He then had 12 points, 6 rebounds, and 5 rebounds on the Washington Wizards. He wrapped that streak up by putting up 14 points and 13 rebounds, which included 5 on the offensive end, versus the Philadelphia 76ers. That was his second double-double game in his career.

Three days later, McGrady scored 16 points and rebounded 9 possessions in 36 minutes of action against the Milwaukee Bucks. He shot 6 out of 11 from the field in that outing. He then had his third double-double as he scored 12 points and collected a then career-high 15 rebounds versus the Miami Heat. Tracy also had five assists, three steals, and two blocks, showing glimpses of his hidden all-around capabilities.

T-Mac would round that three-game streak up with 20 points, 7 rebounds, 6 assists, and 3 steals against the Nets in his second 20-point performance of the season. He shot an efficient 9 out of 13 from the field in that game. In the next match, Tracy had 10 rebounds in a win against the same team but failed to crack into double-digit scoring, as he could only muster up 8 points.

Carter started McGrady for the last 15 games of the season, and McGrady finished the season on a high note, despite Toronto's disappointing season. Since taking over the starting spot, Tracy McGrady had 7 double-digit scoring games out of a possible 15 outings. At that moment, one might think that Tracy McGrady would own that starting role in the next season, as he had already shown flashes of what he could do when given enough minutes. Despite the apparent star potential, it was premature to claim that he would become a superstar in the next few years, as his role did not change as a sophomore player. In his rookie season, Tracy McGrady averaged 7 points, 4 rebounds, and 1.5 assists in 18.4 minutes. For a rookie, he shot a solid 45% from the floor. The Raptors ended up with a record of 16-66 that season.

Of course, the reason why McGrady did not get enough minutes was the fact that there were older players who the coaches wanted to favor more than the teenager. The Raptors' starting shooting guard was the veteran Doug Christie, who was known for his defensive talents. Christie was a no-brainer over McGrady for the starting off-guard spot because of his experience and defensive abilities. But for some reason, the coaches decided to start John Wallace, who was never one of the best players in the NBA, over McGrady at small forward.

In a way, McGrady's role player minutes may have been due to the fact that no coach would risk the ire of veteran players who did not want to see a young teenager getting more minutes than them. But in hindsight, the Raptors should have flirted with the idea of allowing McGrady to start and get his touches because they were not even good enough to compete. Giving McGrady minutes and touches would have actually given him the confidence that he needed to improve as a budding star. But he needed to wait a few more years before actually making the splash that he wanted to make when he chose to forego college to get to the NBA.

## Second Season, Vince Carter's Arrival

If there was an upside to Toronto's season, it was that they managed to obtain the 4th pick in the 1998 NBA Draft. The Raptors would use their pick to obtain swingman Vince Carter. Of course, Carter was another one of the rising and talented wings that could not escape the Michael Jordan comparisons because he went to UNC, the same school that Jordan went to for college. On top of that, Carter was a freakish athlete who dunked on heads in college, just like what Jordan did during his peak years in the NBA. And Carter was even more explosive and athletic compared to T-Mac.

McGrady was excited to play alongside Vince because he was already familiar with him. The two Florida natives had played with and against each other during their teenage years before they discovered that they were, in fact, distant cousins.[x] Vince was older than McGrady, but had played at North Carolina for three years before joining the NBA. The two had plenty to teach each other about basketball and NBA life. They became inseparable, and one Toronto teammate joked that they were "Siamese twins." But the fact that Carter played college basketball and was more prepared to deal with the rigors of the NBA because he was older was the reason why he quickly became the team's top option on offense.

But it took a while before McGrady and Carter could take the court together because the NBA went into a labor-induced lockdown when the team owners and the NBA Players Association had disagreements in relation to their contracts. The talks went on for months until a new Collective Bargaining Agreement (CBA) was struck between the two parties. That was why the 1998-99 season started in February of 1999. The season was shortened to 50 games.

Thanks largely to Carter, the Raptors had their best season in the brief history of their young franchise. They started the season strong and were a serious threat to make the playoffs before fading down the stretch.

As the Raptors focused more on the explosive entry of Vince Carter into the NBA, Tracy McGrady was still left playing role player's minutes off the bench. That season could have been Tracy's breakout season after he showed flashes of brilliance at the tail end of the regular season during his rookie year. However, at that moment, Vince Carter was the more polished, experienced, and mature player. He was already 22 years old. On the other hand, T-Mac was barely 20. The athletic 6'6" rookie would become the team's franchise player while McGrady was off trying to develop into a decent swingman. Nevertheless, T-Mac was still playing better than he did in his rookie year.

McGrady started his second season by scoring 13 points in 13 minutes in an 11-point win against the Boston Celtics. He then scored 14 points in the next game against the Washington Wizards. On February 18, 1999, he would score 14 points as he made 10 out of 12 free throws in a loss to the Wizards once again. After that, he played 28 minutes to score 12 points in a win against the Milwaukee Bucks.

McGrady would have his first double-double of the season with 14 points and 13 rebounds in a 15-point win versus the New Jersey Nets on March 16th. He played 23 minutes that game, shot 6 out of 12 from the field, and had 6 offensive rebounds.

Three days after his first double-double, McGrady had 10 points and 12 rebounds in a big win against the Los Angeles Clippers. He played 29 minutes that game as he shot 2 out of 7 from the field and collected 5 offensive boards. Tracy would establish a season high of 15 points as he shot 7 out of 10 in a loss to the Houston Rockets on March 25th. He would have another double-double performance on April 6th when he had 12 points and 10 rebounds in 26 minutes. He shot 4 out of 8 from the field and had 4 offensive rebounds.

T-Mac would have his first 20-10 game of the season on April 12th. He also established a new season high in that game. He had 21 points on 9 out of 19 shooting. McGrady had 7 offensive rebounds for a total of 10 rebounds in that 10-point loss to the Indiana Pacers. A week later, Tracy bounced back with 16 points and 11 rebounds in an 18-point win against the Orlando Magic. He played 30 minutes that game and had 7 offensive rebounds. He scored 14 points the following night.

McGrady would establish a new season high as the season was about to end. He had 27 points in a loss to the Charlotte Hornets on April 27th. He played 25 minutes that game while shooting 9 out of 12 from the field and 8 out of 8 from the foul stripe. Three days later, he had 19 points and 13 rebounds in a loss to the Cleveland Cavaliers. McGrady ended the regular season scoring 15 points in a win over Cleveland.

McGrady finished his sophomore year averaging 9.3 points, 5.7 rebounds, and 2.3 assists. His scoring improvement could mainly be attributed to the increased minutes he played that season, but his passing and all-around game had developed from a year of playing in the NBA.

McGrady played 22.6 minutes that season, but he did not score a lot of points because the Raptors' offense was focused on Carter. Nevertheless, Tracy was a surprisingly great rebounder that season, as he had almost 6 rebounds per game in barely 23 minutes a night. In that lockout-shortened season, the Raptors won only 23 games and could not qualify for the postseason.

Of course, the reason why McGrady did not get a lot of minutes in his second year in the NBA was the fact that he and Carter shared the same small forward position, and Doug Christie was still the starting shooting guard. Tracy was barely 20 years old at that time and was still learning what it was like to play at that level of basketball. On the other hand, Carter already had three years of college basketball under his belt, and that meant that he had more experience and preparation for the NBA.

Nevertheless, McGrady's per-36 numbers showed that he was incredibly productive despite the fact that he did not get the same touches that Carter and Christie had. He was developing steadily. The problem was that the wing position in Toronto was a little bit too log-jammed for him to make some noise. So, in a way, his cousin may have inadvertently held his development back because Tracy might have actually been given the starting small forward position had the Raptors drafted another player not named Vince Carter.

## Improving Star, First Playoff Season

It was the 1999-2000 season when McGrady finally began to develop into a real star. His overall game continued to improve, especially on the defensive end. While the team was still centered around the ever-rising star of Vince Carter, McGrady was not far behind his cousin in terms of productivity. Tracy played off the bench as the Raptors' sixth man. When he and Vince were both on the floor, the Toronto Raptors would suddenly become a circus of athleticism with high-flying dunks and acrobatic plays.

T-Mac started the season by scoring in double digits in his first four games. After scoring 11 points in the season opener, he had 14, 16, and 14 points in the next three games, which were all blowout wins. The Raptors would win one more game after that as they started 4-1 in their first five games thanks to the high-flying act of McGrady and Carter.

From November 24th to the middle of December in 1999, Tracy McGrady demonstrated that he had finally developed into a capable star player, as he scored in double digits in all of the 11 games he played in that span.

He had 21 points and 8 rebounds in a win over Washington on December 3rd. He then had 21 points, 7 boards, and 6 assists in 31 minutes as the Raptors defeated the Indiana Pacers on December 14th. The following night, he had 18 points, 9 rebounds, and 6 assists in a tight loss to Philadelphia. He finished the 11-game run by scoring 20 points together with 8 rebounds and 6 assists in a big loss to the Orlando Magic.

Shortly after his 11-game scoring streak ended, McGrady started a nine-game run of scoring in double digits. He started that run with a performance of 24 points, 11 rebounds, and 4 assists in a win in Dallas on December 30th. He began the new millennium by scoring 18 points on January 4, 2000, against the Portland Trail Blazers. After that run ended, he started a similar double-digit scoring streak from January 19th to February 16th.

In that streak, Tracy had 5 games of scoring at least 20 points. He had back-to-back 20-point performances against Washington and Miami on January 26th and 28th. He then had 21 points and 6 rebounds in a loss to the Spurs in his first game in February. In a loss to Detroit, he had 20 points and 9 boards. And, because of his high-flying acts, he was a participant in the 2000 Slam Dunk Contest together with Vince Carter. Originally, he did not want to participate because he thought he couldn't beat Carter. But his cousin dragged him to the showcase.

Shortly after the All-Star Break, Coach Carter decided that the time had finally come to make McGrady a full-time starter. Even though

McGrady was 6'8", Carter placed McGrady at the point guard position. It was a sign of how much confidence Carter had in McGrady's ball-handling abilities.

In addition to ball-handling, McGrady made it his mission to shut down the best perimeter player on the opposing team. He described himself as the Scottie Pippen to Vince Carter, said that he had no problems with his role, and played like Pippen when shutting down wings like Grant Hill and an emerging Kobe Bryant.

From that moment on, Tracy McGrady started to blossom into a full-fledged star. McGrady would score in double digits from February 20th up to his final game of the season on April 19th. He never looked back from the moment he took the starting spot.

In his third game as a starter, McGrady had 13 points and 15 rebounds in a win versus the Chicago Bulls. He had a whopping total of 10 offensive rebounds in that game. He then had 18 points and one rebound in his next game. After that, he notched 24 points against the Boston Celtics. He helped his team win seven straight games in that stretch.

McGrady had his second 20-10 game of the season as he recorded 22 points and 12 rebounds in a loss to the Nets on March 21st. He had 7 offensive boards in that game. McGrady scored 20 in the following game. After scoring 24 points on the Indiana Pacers in a 21-point loss on April 2nd, Tracy went for a new career high of 28 points together with 11 rebounds, 5 dimes, and 4 blocks in a loss to the Detroit

Pistons. He would break the 20-point mark two more times as the season ended. He had 27 points, 6 rebounds, 9 assists, 3 steals, and 6 blocks as he paced the way for the Raptors' win against Cleveland on April 10th.

At the end of the season, the Raptors finished with a 45-37 record. They finished with a record above .500 and qualified for the playoffs for the first time in franchise history. McGrady finished averaging 15.4 points, 6.3 rebounds, and 3.3 assists, which were all career highs. He was finally showing signs of his future superstar self as he developed into a good secondary scorer and a great rebounder. McGrady had nine double-doubles since becoming a starter. He was also the Raptor's leading shot blocker that season as he recorded 1.9 blocks per game. Indeed, Tracy was blocking more shots than both of the Raptors' big men combined!

McGrady was primarily used as a defender and rebounder during his third year in the NBA. He could score and finish strong near the basket, especially when he and his cousin were throwing highlight-reel dunks over their defenders. But the Raptors did not give a lot of opportunities to T-Mac to showcase what he could do when he had the ball in his hands and was allowed to generate offense for himself. In that regard, he was mostly defending the opposing team's best wing players, as evidenced by the fact that he had a lot of blocks that season.

T-Mac's efforts were noticed by the league. He was a sixth man for the Raptors, and that was why he was third behind Rodney Rogers and Cuttino Mobley for the Sixth Man of the Year Award.

You could argue that McGrady had better numbers than those players. But the fact was that he started more games than they did, and that was probably the reason why some voters did not give McGrady the award. Still, the important part was that he was now getting better and better. *And* he was on his way to the playoffs at the tender age of 20!

In the first round of the 2000 NBA Playoffs, the Raptors faced off against the New York Knicks. The Knicks were a tough defensive team at that time. Patrick Ewing was not as good as he once was but he remained the emotional bedrock of a New York team that had made the NBA Finals last year. The Knicks were used to the pressures of the playoffs, while the young Raptors were not. New York prevailed over Toronto by sweeping them in three close games.

McGrady played well over the series. He scored 25 points in Game 1, averaged nearly as many points as Vince Carter over the three games, and shot a better percentage from the field as well. While McGrady had his struggles against the Knicks staunch defense, there was no doubt that he could look back on his season without regrets.

But while McGrady had a good third year in the league, it was clear that he was not enjoying his time in Toronto. The Raptors were Vince Carter's squad, and that meant that he was the team's top option on offense. Of course, he had proved himself capable enough to handle

44

the spotlight and carry a team to the playoffs because he averaged nearly 26 minutes a game. But while Carter was building his All-Star resume, T-Mac was often seen sulking on the bench because he did not exactly enjoy the fact that his coach did not trust him to make plays with the ball in his hands. The minutes were there, but he was itching to prove that he also had what it takes to become a franchise player.

The most common problem with having two wing players who could score the ball and make plays at a high level is often related to the fact that they both need the ball in their hands to be effective. What made it worse was that these players were the very same ones who were influenced by Michael Jordan's stardom in the NBA. Every wing player wanted to shoot 20 shots a game and become like Mike when, in fact, someone needed to be like Scottie, who was more than happy to create shots for others instead of generating points for himself. However, both McGrady and Carter were more like Jordan instead of Pippen. And there was only one ball that they needed to share.

## The Move to Orlando; A Breakout Season

The question for Tracy McGrady became what to do next. He was now a free agent. While rookies today have to go through the process of a restricted free agency that helps teams keep their drafted players, no such advantage existed in 2000. While the Raptors management believed that they could re-sign McGrady, the reality was that he had no interest in staying in Toronto.

McGrady was upset by Toronto's offseason decision to fire Coach Carter, and his agent told him that he could make more money playing in the United States instead of Canada. Furthermore, while McGrady had earlier stated that he had no problem being the second wheel to Carter, he was now interested in joining a new team where he could become a franchise player.[xi] By this point, he knew he was just as good as his cousin, if not better. A move elsewhere was the better choice for him as a rising star because he might never come out of Vince Carter's shadow in Toronto.

During the 2000 offseason, the Orlando Magic contacted McGrady. Orlando had once drawn McGrady's interest in basketball with the Shaq-Penny duo, but now both stars were gone. Instead, Orlando now had enough cap space to sign two players to a maximum salaried deal. Orlando initially hoped to get Spurs legend Tim Duncan as well as Detroit Pistons star Grant Hill. But when Duncan decided to stay with the Spurs, the Magic went to Plan B—Tracy McGrady.

McGrady considered his options. He could play for the Chicago Bulls and rising power forward Elton Brand. He could also sign with the Miami Heat and join All-NBA center Alonzo Mourning and legendary coach Pat Riley. Both were intriguing options, however, McGrady eventually leaned toward the Magic. Tracy liked having the chance to play for his hometown team, wanted to play alongside Grant Hill, and was also impressed by Magic coach Doc Rivers.

In 2000, the Toronto Raptors signed on the dotted line and traded McGrady to the Orlando Magic. The young superstar would earn $67 million over six years. Grant Hill signed with the Magic as well for seven years and $90 million. Orlando had established a young dynamic perimeter duo and envisioned a return to the NBA Finals.

But, just as McGrady's first year in Toronto saw the derailment of a promising Raptors team, the Magic quickly ran into trouble. This time, the issue was with an injury to Grant Hill.

Hill had not suffered from any major injury problems in his first six years as a star for the Detroit Pistons. However, toward the end of the 1999-2000 season, he suffered an ankle injury. For various reasons, Hill continued to play on the ankle and eventually broke it during the 2000 NBA Playoffs.

Hill sat out for the rest of the playoffs and focused on his recovery, but the ankle continued to plague him. In the 2000-01 season, his first season with the Orlando Magic, Hill played just 4 ineffective games in the first two months of the NBA season. In late December, he was placed on the injury list and underwent ankle surgery on January 3, 2001. He would miss the rest of the season.

The Magic had spent their cap space on Hill and McGrady, and thus lacked effective players to complement T-Mac once Hill's injury problems began. Their best players were undrafted scoring point guard Darrell Armstrong, who had averaged 16 points for the Magic last season, power forward Bo Outlaw, and a rookie, Mike Miller.

Without McGrady, the Magic would have almost assuredly been one of the worst teams in the league.

Fortunately for the Magic, they *did* have McGrady. If there was an upside to Hill's injury, it was that it permitted McGrady to show just what he could do as the undisputed franchise star. In his first game in a Magic uniform, McGrady played 46 minutes, scored 32 points, and had 12 rebounds and 4 assists as Orlando defeated Washington 97-86.

Nights like that would become the standard for the rising star. McGrady was expected to do everything for the Magic. It was not enough for McGrady to be an efficient scorer—he also had to pass, rebound, play excellent defense, and be there in the clutch when Orlando needed him.

As the Magic's sole superstar, Tracy McGrady had figured himself to score in double digits in almost all his games during the 2000-01 season. In his fourth game in Orlando, he had 31 points, 6 rebounds, 4 assists, 4 steals, and 2 blocks in an 11-point win versus the Seattle Sonics. He broke the 30-point mark one more time on December 1, 2000, before going for a new career high in the next game. He had 40 points, 10 rebounds, 5 assists, 3 steals, and 3 blocks as he virtually did everything to get the 21-point win in New Jersey. He made 18 out of 32 field goals in that game.

McGrady would score at least 30 points in three more games after that 40-point explosion. On December 25th versus the Indiana Pacers in a loss, T-Mac went for his new career best of 43 points along with 9 rebounds. On January 20, 2001, Tracy and the Magic would upset the San Antonio Spurs on their own floor as the burgeoning superstar went for 38 points, 8 rebounds, and 4 assists.

It was on January 23rd that McGrady faced the Toronto Raptors for the first time since he had moved on from that team. He did not have the best scoring performance in that game but he did finish it with 22 points, 7 rebounds, and 7 assists. But, more importantly, McGrady led his team to a win against his former team to prove that he was a gem that the Raptors had allowed to leave.

From January 31st until March 7th, McGrady scored 20 or more points in 17 consecutive games. In the middle of all that, he was nominated to the All-Star Game for the very first time in his career, as he was clearly the sole leader and superstar carrying the Orlando Magic. He would merely score 2 points in his first appearance in the midseason classic. Shortly after the All-Star break, he had a new career high of 44 points in a slim loss to the Phoenix Suns on February 20th. He would score 32 points in the next game as he wrapped up four consecutive games of scoring at least 30 points.

On February 26th, Tracy would go for 36 points and 12 rebounds in a win against the Denver Nuggets. He had 25 points, 12 boards, and 8 dimes in the following game as he narrowly missed what could have been his first career triple-double. He flirted with that stat again on March 13th when he had 25 points, 10 rebounds, and 8 assists.

Tracy would tie his career high of 44 points in a one-point win against the Philadelphia 76ers on March 28th. He also had nine rebounds and six assists in that game. T-Mac would flirt with a triple-double again as he had 34 points, 8 boards, and 11 dimes versus the Boston Celtics on April 4th. Nine days later, McGrady established a new career high as he exploded for 49 points in a slim loss to the Wizards on April 13th. He shot 19 out of 31 from the floor and 9 of 14 from the foul stripe. He also had eight rebounds, seven assists, and four blocks in the 44 minutes he played that game.

McGrady averaged 26.5 points, 7.5 rebounds, and 4.6 assists that season. He finished seventh in the league in scoring, nearly led the Magic in rebounds despite the fact that he was a swingman, and passed and defended just as well as any other wing in the league. He was named to the All-NBA second team in that season as he established himself as one of the top perimeter players in the whole NBA.

McGrady's gaudy numbers also led to wins, as the Magic managed to win 43 games and return to the playoffs after missing it in 2001. They would face the Milwaukee Bucks in the first round.

Milwaukee had no single player that was as good as McGrady. Still, the Bucks had three stars in Sam Cassell, Ray Allen, and Glenn Robinson, who all had depth and were coached by all-time great George Karl. If McGrady wanted to win, he would need to beat the heavily favored Bucks practically by himself.

In his first playoff game as a Magic, McGrady had 9 rebounds and assists. However, he struggled to score—while he scored 33 points, he shot 34 times. The Bucks would win Game 1 and 2, and it looked like it would be an easy sweep for the better team.

However, McGrady answered with an incredible performance in Game 3. In an overtime game, he scored 42 points along with 10 assists and 8 rebounds. He also hit several key shots in the fourth quarter and overtime as Orlando prevailed in Game 3. Milwaukee would end the series at Game 4, but the Magic would remain hopeful. They had proven that McGrady was a superstar. With Grant Hill back and healthy, they would be ready to make some noise.

But while the Magic was banking on Hill's return, it was McGrady's surprising rise as a star that turned heads. He was just barely 22 years old at that time but had become one of the brightest young stars in the entire NBA. Not a lot of people expected him to become this good because the expectation was that he was just going to play behind a healthy Grant Hill instead of actually playing like a true superstar. And head coach Doc Rivers was not even expecting T-Mac to be this good.

"Much better," Rivers said when asked about whether he expected McGrady to be so good. "I thought he would be a great defensive player, handle the ball for us. I didn't know he could shoot. He didn't get any shots in Toronto, so none of us knew. He may be a better scorer than Vince. I think he's more difficult to guard, and I would have never thought that."[xii]

In a way, Doc did not know that McGrady was going to be as good as he was during the 2000-01 season because he did not see him getting the shots that he should have been getting back in Toronto. This was a clear indication that the Raptors' coaching staff did not allow him to get shots off despite his immense talent. It might be an internal feud between McGrady and his former coaches, but the fact that Rivers was not aware that he could shoot and generate points for himself off the dribble was proof that he was underutilized while he was in Toronto. Apparently, all that he had needed was to find the team that would give him the ultimate green light on offense. Of course, his green light came almost by accident—on the heels of Hill's injury—but it was an eye-opening, triumphant point in Grady's career nonetheless.

McGrady's ceiling was now higher than ever because he had proven himself a true star in every sense of the word. He was a wasted talent in Toronto, especially because the coaches failed to find a way for him to have the same kind of opportunities and touches that Carter was getting. In that sense, the Raptors might have been able to have two great players in Carter and McGrady if they had not pulled the plug on the T-Mac experiment so early. But now, McGrady was in a situation that allowed him to truly be at his best. Still, no one was expecting him to eventually become one of the true elites of the game.

# Carrying the Magic Load Once Again

Despite high expectations, the 2001-02 season remained more of the same for Orlando. Hill played just 14 games before once again undergoing ankle surgery. The Magic brought in aging veterans like Horace Grant and a 39-year-old Patrick Ewing but failed once again to give McGrady a proper supporting cast. Because of those setbacks, Tracy McGrady was set to carry the Orlando Magic on his 22-year-old shoulders for yet another season.

Tracy would start the 2001-02 season slowly until he scored 44 points and grabbed 13 rebounds in his sixth game of the season. He shot 14 out of 30 from the field that game as he led the Magic to a 10-point win. As defenses keyed in on McGrady that season, he no longer had the element of surprise on his side, unlike in his breakout season in 2000-01. Nevertheless, he went for 39 points, 7 boards, and 8 assists in an 11-point win against the Timberwolves on November 21, 2001.

On December 8th and 10th, Tracy McGrady had back-to-back 40-point double-double games. He first had 40 points and 11 rebounds against the Atlanta Hawks. He then had 47 points and 11 boards against the Los Angeles Clippers. However, both games were losses. Two games later on December 13th, he went for 40 in a win against the Golden State Warriors.

At the end of January 2002, T-Mac had three straight games of double-doubles. He had 17 points and 11 rebounds before going for an average of 24.5 and 10 rebounds in the next two games. For the

53

second straight season, McGrady was selected to play in the All-Star Game. In that year's edition of the midseason classic, Tracy McGrady scored 24 points on 9 out of 15 shooting.

Shortly after the All-Star break, McGrady had his first career triple-double on February 23rd. He had 22 points, 11 rebounds, and 11 assists as the Magic defeated the Philadelphia 76ers by 18 points. On March 8th, McGrady established a new career high as he went for 50 points together with 10 rebounds in a win against the Washington Wizards. He shot 18 out of 29 from the field and 10 out of 15 from the free throw line. From that moment, he led the Magic to six straight wins.

In the middle of that winning streak, Tracy had 29 points and 13 assists against the 76ers. He then had 48 points and 12 rebounds in the next game against the Bucks. In that explosion, T-Mac shot 18 out of 35 from the field and 6 out of 9 from three-point range. McGrady would end the season the right way by scoring at least 30 points in five of his next 13 games. He also had five double-doubles in that span.

McGrady averaged 25.6 points, 7.9 rebounds, 5.3 assists, and 1.6 steals in his second year with the Orlando Magic. He was named to the All-NBA first team because T-Mac was, at least for that moment, the best shooting guard in the whole NBA. That was something huge because it meant that he was better than Carter, Bryant, and Iverson in that season. He almost single-handedly led the Magic to a record of

44-38, which was good enough for the fifth seed in the Eastern Conference playoff picture.

The Orlando Magic would face the Charlotte Hornets in the first round of the playoffs. In Game 1 of that matchup, T-Mac struggled against the Hornets' defense as he was limited to 20 points on 8 out of 21 shooting. Had he made just one more field goal, they would have won that game, as the Magic lost by merely a point. McGrady would bounce back in Game 2 when he scored 31 points together with 11 rebounds, 7 assists, 2 steals, and 3 blocks. In the 48 minutes he played in that overtime game, McGrady shot 11 out of 23 from the field and 9 out of 12 from the foul line. Orlando won that game by eight points.

Tracy McGrady would perform spectacularly in Game 3. In that overtime game, he had 37 points and 7 rebounds. He shot 11 out of 25 from the floor in the 51 minutes he played. Unfortunately, the Magic could not perform in overtime as the Hornets outscored them by 10 in the extra period.

As Orlando was down 2-1 heading into Game 4, it was up to McGrady once again to try to bail them out. Unfortunately, the one-man show would not work against the balanced offense of Charlotte and the Magic lost that one by 17. Tracy McGrady had 35 points and 6 assists in that outing.

Despite losing in the first round once more, it became apparent that McGrady had become one of the truly elite wing players in the entire NBA. He was playing the shooting guard position but was given a forward slot in the All-NBA first team, where he shared the wing spot with Kobe Bryant. But while Bryant was the more accomplished player of the two, it was clear that the difference between them was not that wide.

There were those who argued that T-Mac was actually better than Kobe on an individual level because he was bigger. On top of that, some critics were saying that Bryant was lucky that he played alongside Shaquille O'Neal. So, if they were to trade places, there might have been a good chance that McGrady would have won the three NBA titles that Bryant had won at that point in his career.

But while it may be true that they were rivals in terms of their individual abilities at the wing position, Tracy and Kobe respected one another and were actually good friends off the court. And Kobe respected T-Mac so much that he eventually said that he was the hardest player that he had to guard.

"There's a lot of guys but the guy that always gave me the most problems, actually was Tracy McGrady," Bryant said in an interview. "He had all the skills and all the athleticism, but he was 6'9" and he was really tough to figure out."[xiii]

This was the ultimate sign of respect because Kobe knew talent when he saw it. It is well known that Bryant studied his opponents methodically and obsessively to understand how to guard them. That meant that he knew his opponent's moves and tendencies. The fact that he said McGrady was the toughest player he ever had to guard was a testament to the talent level that T-Mac had during the prime of his career. Tracy was so good and so dominant as a scorer that he gave one of the greatest players of all time trouble on the defensive end. And we all know that Bryant was one of the greatest defensive wings in the history of the NBA.

But while McGrady had already reached elite status in the league, he was not yet done. He still had a lot more memories to make as a dominant scorer in the NBA. The world was not ready for what T-Mac had in store in the following season, as this was his true peak as an NBA superstar.

## Back-to-Back Scoring Championships

While McGrady had been an impressive shooting guard for the past two seasons, his 2002-03 performance is arguably the greatest single season ever by a shooting guard not named Jordan or Bryant. In addition to ferociously driving the ball to the rim, McGrady improved his three-point shot and his ball handling. With Grant Hill limited to merely 29 games that season, it was up to Tracy once again to score big for the Orlando Magic, particularly since the only other scorer on that team was Mike Miller.

T-Mac opened the season with 31 points, 4 rebounds, 5 assists, and 4 blocks in a win over Philadelphia. On November 2nd and 5th, McGrady went four consecutive games of scoring at least 40 points. He first had 47 points, 6 rebounds, and 7 dimes on the Milwaukee Bucks. In that win, he shot 16 out of 29 from the floor and 9 out of 9 from the foul stripe. He played 38 minutes in that game. In the next matchup, he had 41 points, 8 boards, and 7 assists against Sacramento. He shot 15 out of 27 from the field in that win.

Shortly after that, McGrady went for seven straight games of scoring at least 30 points. In the middle of that, he had 36 points, 14 rebounds, and 7 assists in a loss to the Kings on November 17th. He then went for 41 points, 12 rebounds, and 4 blocks in a win in Seattle. One game after the streak ended, Tracy went for 38 points in a win against Bryant and the Los Angeles Lakers. He matched Kobe, who also had 38 points in that game.

On December 25th, McGrady gifted the Magic with 46 points and a win versus the Pistons. T-Mac shot 14 out of 26 from the field in that game, and 18 out of 21 from the free throw line. He followed up that performance by scoring 35 points in the next match. In a loss to the New Orleans Hornets on January 3, 2003, T-Mac went for 40 points once again as he made 14 out of 29 field goals.

From January 16th to February 2nd, Tracy went for eight straight games of scoring 30 or more points. He also had four double-doubles in that span, which included two subsequent ones. He had 35 points and 11 rebounds in each win in Toronto and Cleveland. He then had 33 points and 11 assists in a narrow loss to the Phoenix Suns. He then had 31 points and 12 rebounds versus the Cleveland Cavaliers. He ended that streak by scoring 38 points against the Atlanta Hawks in an eight-point loss. McGrady would go for his third All-Star appearance in that season.

On February 23rd, McGrady notched his second career triple-double. Moreover, that was a phenomenal scoring game. He had 46 points, 10 rebounds, and 13 assists in a win against the New Jersey Nets. He shot 16 out of 27 from the floor and 11 out of 13 from the foul stripe. That performance was just two days after he scored a career-high 52 points against the Chicago Bulls. He had 15 out of 32 field goals in that game as well as 16 out of 20 from the free throw line. Tracy made six three-pointers that game.

McGrady would then go on a 14-game streak of scoring at least 30 points. He had four games of scoring 40 or more points in that high-scoring streak. On March 5th, he had 48 points and 10 rebounds against the Milwaukee Bucks. He made six three-point shots in that game. He then had consecutive 43-point games versus the Denver Nuggets and the Washington Wizards. McGrady combined for 29 out of 50 from the field in those two games as well as dropping 10 out of 18 from beyond the arc. As his streak was nearing its end, he had 41 points versus the Hornets. Tracy went 14 out of 28 from the floor in that game.

At the end of the regular season, McGrady averaged 32.1 points, 6.5 rebounds, 5.5 assists, and 1.7 steals. He shot a career-best 45.7% from the floor and 38.6% from the three-point line. He won the scoring championship that season as well, notably beating Kobe Bryant in that regard by 2.1 points.

McGrady joined the likes of Wilt Chamberlain, Michael Jordan, David Robinson, and Shaquille O'Neal as one of only seven players in NBA history to have a player efficiency rating (PER) of 30 or more. And Jordan was the last guard to have a PER of 30 or more, as most of the other players who were able to reach that level of efficiency in the NBA were big men who could stuff the stats sheet with their scoring, rebounding, and shot-blocking.

One of the reasons why T-Mac was able to score a lot of points and lead the NBA in PER was the fact that he was a trailblazing wing who shot a lot of three-pointers as a designated top option on offense. McGrady finished the season behind only Ray Allen, Antoine Walker, Michael Redd, and Allan Houston. But unlike all the above mentioned names, he was not a spot-up shooter who relied on roaming around the perimeter for his teammates to find. Instead, he generated his shots all on his own, as there was no other player on the Magic who could make plays on a consistent basis.

So, in short, a lot of the three-pointers that McGrady took were taken off the dribble and against the outstretched arms of his defender. He was essentially Kevin Durant before Durant even got to college. That was because McGrady had the ability to shoot tough shots over his defenders without even flinching. His shot-making ability was off the charts, and there was a reason why some fans thought that he may have actually been a better individual talent than Kobe Bryant at that time during his absolute peak.

T-Mac was so good that season that he had 11 games of scoring at least 40 points. That included one game of scoring beyond 50. McGrady, for the second straight season, was named the best shooting guard in the league as he was first team All-NBA. He led the Magic to a record of 42-40. But because the Magic were merely the eighth seed in the Eastern Conference heading into the postseason, McGrady could not win the MVP.

The 2003 MVP Award went to Tim Duncan, who had led his team to 60 wins. McGrady did not even finish in the top three of the MVP voting because Garnett and Bryant were ahead of him in terms of votes. Of course, Duncan deserved the award because he had the highest win shares out of all the players who ended up getting votes for the MVP. But T-Mac was only second to him in win shares, and was *first* in win shares per 48 minutes. Simply put, McGrady was the only reason why the Orlando Magic were in the playoffs that season. Without him, the Magic would have easily been a lottery team. And it was during those playoffs that T-Mac showed that he should have finished at least third in the MVP voting.

Tracy McGrady made an immediate explosion in the first round of the playoffs, recording 43 points and 7 rebounds in an upset win over the top-seeded Detroit Pistons. He would next score 46 points in Game 2 as the Pistons' defense could not solve him. However, Detroit won that game by 12 points. McGrady scored 29 points in a win in Game 3 when the series moved over to Orlando. He then led the Magic to a 3-1 lead in the series with 27 points, 9 assists, and 5 steals in Game 4.

After Game 4, Tracy McGrady prematurely announced to the world that he was sure the Magic would proceed to the second round by saying, "It feels good to get into the second round."

However, that would not be the case, as the Detroit Pistons got their act together to win the next three games. All three games were blowout wins for the Pistons. Tracy was limited to a combined 26 out of 72 from the field in those three losses, as the Pistons' defense finally found a way to stop the scoring champion from exploding.

After losing those three straight games, Tracy McGrady probably felt like he had jinxed his team with his premature boast. For the fourth time in his career, McGrady was ousted from the first round of the postseason. But despite the early exit from the playoffs, McGrady had finally broken out as probably the best perimeter player in the NBA at that time.

However, relations between McGrady and the Magic began to deteriorate. In March 2003, Grant Hill had suffered a serious infection due to surgery complications, and thus was declared out for the entire 2003-04 season, and McGrady had had enough. He was starting to battle back problems from having to do it all on his own. While being the franchise player had been fun in 2000, he was tired of carrying a sub-par team to first round exits again and again. He wanted help and he wanted it fast. Unfortunately, no help came. In fact, the entire Magic team suffered from injury problems during the 2003-04 season. Because of that, Tracy had to steer a sinking ship once again.

The Orlando Magic was far from being one of the best-run organizations in the NBA at that time. The team never had the best luck in terms of its superstars, and the way that the franchise handled problems with their best players was probably a lesson in how *not* to run an NBA team. In the past, they failed to keep Shaquille O'Neal, who wanted to be in a bigger city. Meanwhile, Penny Hardaway also had his own issues with the Magic before his own body eventually deteriorated due to injuries. And Grant Hill was a big "what-if" story for the Magic because he had only stayed healthy enough to play a total of 47 games for Orlando at that point in his career, and he was probably not even 100% in most of those games.

No one could ever blame McGrady for being unhappy with his situation in Orlando. It was apparent to all that the team just did not have the best luck, and furthermore, they were not entirely the best at making decisions during the offseason when it came to seeking players who could help reduce McGrady's offensive load. Playing 40 minutes a night while shooting more than 20 attempts over physical defenders was tough for McGrady and the stress on his body was significant. But he had no choice because he was the only player on that team capable of generating offense on a regular basis.

T-Mac was once again a one-man show during the 2003-04 season. He started the season by scoring 33 and 31 in his second and third game. He then had 36 points against the Memphis Grizzlies on November 12, 2003, as he shot 14 out of 26 from the floor. In the next game, he exploded for 51 big points on the Denver Nuggets. He made 20 out of 30 from the floor in that game and made 8 three-point shots. But despite his hot start, McGrady could not translate those achievements into wins for the team. The Orlando Magic lost 19 straight games at the beginning of the season. Doc Rivers was fired in the middle of all that.

It was not Rivers' fault that the Magic were losing. The team simply did not have a roster that was built to win. McGrady was already operating at peak capacity just to make sure the team was given a chance to compete night in and night out. But with Juwan Howard as his second-best player (who would one day become a far better coach at the college level than he ever was as a player in the NBA), there was not a lot that Rivers could have done to save that sinking ship. Essentially, Doc was a scapegoat for the team's lack of success. And on McGrady's part, he was now forced to carry a team that did not even have the head coach that had helped him become one of the premiere scorers in the entire league.

Despite the losing record, T-Mac still tried his best to play at a high level. He had 10 straight games of scoring at least 20 points in December. He also had three double-doubles in that span. In a Christmas Day matchup against the Cleveland Cavaliers, McGrady defeated LeBron James' team by scoring 41 points and grabbing 11 rebounds in overtime. He made 15 out of 29 shots from the floor in that outing.

On January 6, 2004, McGrady went for 40 or more once again as he scored 43 points in a loss to the Indiana Pacers. Ten days later, he scored 44 in a win against the Boston Celtics. Those performances were in the middle of a 21-game streak of scoring at least 20 points. McGrady was chosen as an All-Star for the fourth straight season.

In the middle of that 21-game scoring streak, T-Mac had 33 points, 10 rebounds, and 6 assists in a win against the Philadelphia 76ers on January 23rd. He then had 39 points in a win versus the Wizards on January 28th. Tracy would end his scoring streak with back-to-back games of breaking the 40-point mark. He had 41 points on February 17th as he shot 15 out of 31 against the Milwaukee Bucks. He then had 43 points as he made 14 free throws in a win against the Utah Jazz the next night.

Though the season seemed unsalvageable for the Orlando Magic, Tracy McGrady continued to pour it on with everything he had. On March 10, 2004, McGrady became only the 11th player in NBA history at that time to score at least 60 points. He had a total of 62 points and 10 rebounds in a win over the Wizards. McGrady made 20 out of 37 shots from the field and 17 out of 26 from the foul line. As an encore performance, he had 40 in his next game. However, T-Mac would be sidelined after his final game of the season on March 24th because of foot injuries. And it turned out that that 18-point performance in a loss to the Miami Heat would be his final game for the Orlando Magic.

At the end of the regular season, McGrady was once again the league's leading scorer with an average of 28 points. He also had 6 rebounds, 5.5 assists, and 1.4 steals. He was named to the All-NBA second team. The Orlando Magic would end the season with a record of 21-61. That was easily the worst record in the NBA that season. Because they finished with such a terrible record, the Orlando Magic won the draft lottery and ended up with the top overall pick, which turned out to be Dwight Howard.

However, the team's decision to select Howard angered Tracy. While we know today that Howard would eventually become a superstar center, in 2004, Howard was viewed as a risky prospect who could have been the next Kwame Brown. Furthermore, since Howard had jumped from high school to the NBA like McGrady had, he would likely need years to develop into a great player. McGrady was unwilling to wait, and he asked for a trade.

Several teams were interested in McGrady, but he was most interested in becoming a Laker. The Lakers had just lost to the Pistons in the NBA Finals, and Kobe Bryant and Shaquille O'Neal had imploded as a duo. One of the two had to go. In the end, O'Neal was the one who left Los Angeles instead of Kobe. Had it been Kobe who was shipped out, the Lakers would have been interested in making a move for

Tracy. Nevertheless, on June 29, 2004, Tracy McGrady, together with three other players, was traded to the Houston Rockets in exchange for capable scorers Cuttino Mobley and Steve Francis. McGrady then signed an extension with the Rockets that would pay him at superstar levels until 2010.

The Magic eventually did well in the years that followed McGrady's departure because Dwight Howard ended up becoming a star center and, at one point, the best big man in the entire NBA. On the flip side, T-Mac was given a chance to shine with a budding star in Yao Ming in Houston. So, in a sense, it was a win-win situation for both teams. But in hindsight, McGrady might have done a lot more if he had stayed in Orlando and played with Dwight Howard. After all, Howard eventually led the Magic to the NBA Finals in 2009.

## First Season in Houston

The Rockets had an immediate superstar for McGrady to play with that the Magic did not. Center Yao Ming had shown great potential in his first two years and had helped lead the Rockets to an eighth seed during the previous season. At the start of the 2004-05 season, Yao and McGrady were 24 and 25, respectively. There was no doubt that, eventually, the two could unite to lead the Rockets to a championship. The two created an inside-outside duo that could have rivaled the Shaq and Kobe combo that Los Angeles had.

However, while Yao Ming was healthy for the time being, unlike Grant Hill, the Rockets, like the Magic, suffered from a lack of support to complement the two stars. Bit players like Bobby Sura and Juwan Howard filled out the rest of the team. In addition to the lack of talent, the supporting players had no potential to get better. The fact of the matter was, the Rockets were *old*. Indeed, no one else on the Rockets who played more than 30 games was less than 28 years old, and the vast majority of players on the team were in their 30s.

The lack of a supporting cast, as well as the necessity of Yao and McGrady learning to play alongside one another, meant that the Rockets struggled at first. It took them 35 games to permanently place themselves above .500. However, McGrady was excellent. He was still the superstar that had dominated the NBA when he was in Orlando.

McGrady scored 18 points in his first game as a Rocket. His breakout game in a red uniform came in his third game of the 2004-05 season when he scored 30 points and had 9 assists in a win versus the Memphis Grizzlies. On November 20, 2004, he had 32 points in a win against the Los Angeles Clippers. McGrady also had seven points and five assists in that game.

In an overtime loss to the Dallas Mavericks, McGrady scored 48 points and flirted with a triple-double with 9 rebounds and 9 assists. He shot 19 out of 32 from the field including 6 out of 13 from beyond the arc in that game. But that was not the highlight of McGrady's 2004 season.

On December 9, 2004, the Rockets took on the eventual champions, the San Antonio Spurs. The Spurs defense throttled Houston for most of the game and led by 10 points with just 55 seconds left. But, as it turned out, 55 seconds was all that T-Mac needed.

At that moment, a sort of scoring demon possessed Tracy McGrady as he took over the game. The Rockets had almost given up in that match, but Tracy hit a three-pointer to cut the lead down to seven. The Rockets then played the fouling game as they continuously gave the ball to their superstar shooting guard. McGrady hit two more three-pointers, including a four-point play, to cut the lead down to two points. He then stole the ball and hit a three-pointer with less than two seconds left to give the 81-80 result to Houston. The Rockets ended up winning that game because McGrady scored 13 points in merely 35 seconds. In 2010, TNT would nominate that game as one of the best regular season performances in the past decade.

To this day, this performance by T-Mac remains one of the most spectacular, mind-boggling feats in the history of the NBA because it is incredibly rare for any player to score at least ten points in under a minute. But McGrady scored 13 points in a little over 30 seconds while leading his team to a stunning comeback win.

He may not have been the most successful player in the postseason, but McGrady was clutch and was capable of hitting impossible shots when the game was on the line. There was a reason why Kobe Bryant called him the hardest player to guard, as he could get a good shot off of any kind of defense. He was a true superstar.

McGrady would not stop playing at the level of a superstar. On December 20th, he had 34 points, 12 rebounds, and 7 assists as the Houston Rockets defeated the Toronto Raptors. Tracy would end the year by scoring 42 points and rebounding 10 possessions for a December 31st win against the Milwaukee Bucks. He played 47 minutes in that game as he contributed to a 15-point win.

The scoring explosions continued into the New Year. T-Mac would have 45 points and 12 rebounds in an 18-point victory versus the Denver Nuggets on January 9, 2005. He shot 15 out of 26 from the field and 10 out of 14 from the free throw line in that game. He followed up that performance with 30 points and 11 rebounds in a win against the Dallas Mavericks in the next match.

McGrady would score 20 or more points in 13 games starting on January 15th. In the middle of that stretch, he had five games of scoring at least 30 points, four of which were victories. He had 35 points in a one-point win versus the Knicks on January 21st. He then scored 33 versus the Hornets in his next game before scoring 30 points and collecting 12 assists in a loss to the Kings. On February 2nd, he contributed 34 points and nine dimes to a 23-point blowout win against the 76ers. Two nights later, he scored 40 points and grabbed 13 rebounds in a six-point win versus the Milwaukee Bucks. He made 14 out of 18 free throws in that game. Shortly after that game, Tracy McGrady was selected to his fifth straight All-Star game appearance.

The Rockets' star shooting guard would not slow down after the midseason break. He went on to score 30 or more points in 10 more outings. He had 32 points and 10 boards against the Dallas Mavericks in a 21-point win versus the Mavs on March 6th. He then scored 35 and 38 in the next two games as he led the Rockets to six straight victories. He would then score 31 in a 19-point blowout against the Cleveland Cavaliers on March 24th. T-Mac would then explode for 44 points and five steals in a 14-point win versus the Jazz. He was ultra-efficient in that game as he shot 15 out of 21 from the field and 11 out of 16 from the free throw line. He next lit up the Golden State Warriors for the same amount of points on April 11th. He made 18 out of 34 shots from the field in that game. However, the Rockets lost that game.

As the team chemistry of the Rockets improved, the team's record improved as well. They went on multiple winning streaks, including a seven-game streak to finish out the season, and finished with 51 wins. It was Houston's highest win total since 1997.

While McGrady did not win the scoring championship for the third straight year, he still averaged 25.7 points, 6.2 rebounds, and 5.7 assists for the season. T-Mac was named to the All-NBA third team. He was the Rockets' leading scorer as they went on to win 51 out of

82 games in the regular season. Houston was the fifth seed in the Western Conference heading into the postseason.

In the first round of the NBA Playoffs, the Rockets battled the rival Dallas Mavericks. McGrady had to do nearly everything for Houston in the series. He scored above 30 points on 45% shooting, passed, rebounded, and even defended Dallas star Dirk Nowitzki by himself. Whenever he came to the bench to rest, Houston collapsed. Yao Ming also played well, but he struggled with foul trouble throughout the series. The rest of the Rockets were mostly ineffective.

Houston managed to win the first two games of the series in Dallas. T-Mac scored 34 and 28 in those games as he shot a combined 24 out of 46 from the field. In Game 2, McGrady ferociously dunked on Dallas center Shawn Bradley and hit the game-winner. He also had 8 rebounds and 10 assists in that match. However, the Mavericks won the next two games in Houston.

Despite the losses in those games, Tracy did well, scoring an average of 32 points on 23 out of 49 shooting in those games in Houston. However, he would have his worst shooting performance of the series as he made only 7 out of 22 from the field in Game 3 for 25 points. Dallas won that tight one by just three points.

Hoping for a miracle from their superstar, the Houston Rockets banked on McGrady once again to force Game 7. He had 37 points on 14 out of 28 shooting to give the Rockets an 18-point win. He also had eight boards and seven dimes in that game. However, the series

72

ended in an utter blowout as Dallas drubbed Houston 116-76. Despite his excellent performances throughout the series, McGrady was criticized for once again coming up short in Game 7.

McGrady was a phenomenal scoring talent. There was no doubt about that. He was a transcendental player at his peak, and he knew how to carry a team on his back. But the problem was that he just did not deliver during the playoffs because he had yet to make it past the first round, no matter how talented a superstar he was. In Orlando, he could be forgiven for not being able to lead his team past the first round because the Magic did not have anyone else who could produce consistently. But there were supposed to be no more excuses for him in Houston because the Rockets had another star in the form of Yao Ming. Nevertheless, the trend remained the same for T-Mac, regardless of where he played.

## Injury-Plagued Season

The Rockets came into the 2005-06 season with high expectations, but the season was derailed by injuries—a grim omen for what was to come for the Yao-McGrady duo. McGrady had suffered from mild back issues when playing for the Magic, but his back turned from a nuisance to a severe problem that season. McGrady missed eight games early in the season because of those back issues. Nevertheless, his play was still at a level needed of a superstar.

On November 12, 2005, Tracy had 35 points and 10 boards in an 8-point win versus the New Jersey Nets. He then had 35, 35, and 34 points in three of Houston's five-game winning stretch early in December. On December 28th, Tracy McGrady exploded for 38 points, 8 boards, and 7 assists against New Orleans/Oklahoma City. However, the Rockets lost that one by two points.

In his first game in January, McGrady had 38 points, 6 rebounds, 5 dimes, and 3 blocks in a 12-point win versus the Washington Wizards. The next game was a win in Cleveland on January 5, 2006, where he had 34 points. He finished that five-game streak of scoring 30 or more with 37 points in a loss to the Toronto Raptors. Despite his good performances, McGrady injured his back again in a game against Denver on January 8th. He had to be taken to the hospital.

Tracy made his return on January 20th in a win in Chicago. He had 35 points in that game and shot 13 out of 29 from the field. He also had nine rebounds and six assists in that match. After that, McGrady would score 40 or more points in two consecutive games. He had 43 points in a loss to Detroit on January 22nd. He made 17 out of 33 field goal attempts in that game. On the following day, he had 41 points in an easy win against the Bucks. He was 17 out of 32 from the floor in that blowout game. On January 29th, T-Mac would have 37 points and 12 boards in a loss to the Miami Heat.

On February 3rd, Tracy scored 36 points in a 23-point blowout versus the Sonics. That would be his final game of scoring 30 or more points in that season. McGrady was chosen as an All-Star for the sixth straight season that year. However, he seemed to slow down after the midseason break, as he never had a chance to score tons of points because of all the injuries that were ailing him at that point. On March 8th, he landed on his back in a game against the Indiana Pacers. He left the game and never returned to the court that season.

In addition to McGrady's injury concerns, Yao Ming missed 25 games with leg injuries. The Rockets were unable to function with both Yao and McGrady absent. McGrady averaged 24.4 points, 6.5 rebounds, and 4.8 assists in 47 games that season. It was evident that injuries were slowing him down as he shot a mere 40.6% from the floor. The Rockets won just 34 games that season and missed the playoffs.

If there was one thing that had become clear about Tracy McGrady, it was that his body was deteriorating rapidly for a man who should have still been in the prime of his career. He was just 26 years old at that point, and that meant that his body should have still been strong enough to heal. But for whatever reason—perhaps the accumulated stress on his body that his playing style demanded—the injuries he suffered that season eventually ended up slowing him down and causing even more injuries in the future. And the fact that he had to carry an entire franchise on his back for four years may have sped up his body's rapid deterioration as well.

## Final All-Star Season

Fortunately for the Rockets, their poor season meant that they had the 8th pick in the 2006 NBA Draft. They traded the pick for veteran

Shane Battier, who would play the supporting role better than the other Rockets player because he was the perfect three-and-D player in the sense that he excelled at defending opposing players and hitting three-pointers.

As the 2006-07 season began, McGrady's back problems initially flared up again, but after further treatment, he managed to finally overcome that problem. He went back to playing as well as he did in 2004-05. When Yao broke his knee in December and missed 34 games, McGrady kept Houston afloat while Yao recovered.

In his first game since coming back from the back injury he suffered in March 2006, T-Mac had 25 points in a loss to the Jazz. In his first 20 games of the season, McGrady seemed to still be bothered by his back, as his scoring slowed down. He would only have two games of scoring 30 or more points in that span. He even had three outings of scoring below 10 points. Despite that, he still played the role of an all-around superstar to prime form as he was able to get four double-doubles in his first 20 games.

Tracy McGrady ended 2006 on a good note as he scored 38 points and grabbed 9 boards in a tight win against the Memphis Grizzlies on December 31st. As 2007 began, McGrady found new life. He scored 31 points in his first game of the New Year, a win in Seattle. He then had 44 points on January 5, 2007, in a win versus the Utah Jazz. He made 14 out of 31 field goals and 13 out of 16 free throws that game.

He would score 31 points in the next two games as the Houston Rockets were still winning games without their 7'6" gigantic center.

On January 13th, T-Mac had 37 points and 9 boards in a four-point win in Sacramento. In the next match, he exploded for 45 big points on 17 out of 29 shooting from the floor and 7 out of 9 from the foul line. However, they lost to the Dallas Mavericks by 13 that game. Eight days later, McGrady had 37 points in a win versus the Spurs. He ended January on a high note by scoring 36 points and collecting 9 dimes in a win versus the SuperSonics on January 31st.

At the start of February, T-Mac had back-to-back games of scoring 30 or more. He had 32 in a big win against the Timberwolves. The night after that, McGrady had 33 in Memphis as he led the Rockets to an 8-point win. Tracy McGrady would be named to his seventh consecutive All-Star game. Unfortunately for him and his fans, that was his last appearance in the midseason classic.

Shortly after the break, Tracy scored at least 30 points in three consecutive games. McGrady had 32 in a 10-point win against Miami on February 21st. Two days later, he scored 37 in a loss to the Hawks. Finally, he went back home to Orlando to score 34 in that win. As the season was about to end, T-Mac scored 40 points together with 8 rebounds and 10 assists in a win versus the Sacramento Kings on April 8th. He had 8 boards and 10 dimes as he flirted with a triple-double. In his final game of the season, Tracy had another near triple-double as he scored 39 points, collected 11 rebounds, and assisted on 9 baskets. Houston won that game by three against the Suns.

At the end of the season, Tracy McGrady averaged 24.6 points, 5.3 rebounds, and 6.5 assists. He was a member of the All-NBA second team for the third time in his career. He almost singlehandedly led the Houston Rockets to a record of 52 wins against 30 losses, finishing the regular season as the fifth seed in the Western Conference playoff bracket. Although he did not win the award, McGrady was a serious contender for the MVP because Yao Ming had missed 34 games that season. They met the Utah Jazz in the first round of the postseason.

Utah proved to be a difficult matchup for the Rockets. Shane Battier was an excellent wing defender by all accounts, but the Jazz relied more on point guard Deron Williams and power forward Carlos Boozer to score instead of their wings. Yao played well offensively but struggled to defend the faster Jazz big man Mehmet Okur, who dwelled outside the three-point line, and Boozer, who shot perimeter jumpers at a high level. The series was an ugly, defense-first battle, so Houston needed McGrady's scoring more than ever.

Tracy was successful and scored above 25 points for the series. McGrady scored 23 points as he helped the Rockets win Game 1 by nine. He then had 31 markers and 10 boards in Game 2 to help his team get to a 2-0 series lead. However, Utah won Games 3 and 4 as Tracy McGrady combined for 42 points on 15 out of 41 shooting in those two losses. He then fought back to score 26 points and dish out 16 assists to help the Rockets take back the series lead.

Utah defended T-Mac well in Game 6 as they forced him to shoot 8 out of 23 from the floor. The Jazz won that one by 12. However, in Game 7, Yao proved unable to stop Carlos Boozer, who dropped 35 points and 14 rebounds to devastating effect. Utah prevailed 103-99 and won the series.

T-Mac had 29 points and 13 assists in that game as he tried his best to lead his team past the first round. If he had won that match, it could have been his first second-round appearance. But that was not the case.

Afterward, a tearful McGrady shrugged his shoulders to the media and declared, "I tried."

McGrady did indeed try his best. There was no shame in not making it out of the first round once more because he proved that he did indeed try to push his team past the first round against a very serious and competitive Jazz team. But there were other problems that were beyond McGrady's control. So, as great of a franchise star as he may have been, he was still human in the sense that he could not do everything for his team. And it eventually turned out that the burden of having to carry his teams for so many years got to him.

# Final Run of a Superstar Shooting Guard

Tracy McGrady would try again for what was to be his final superstar season. Houston management finally began to get Yao and McGrady the supporting teammates that they needed. Rookie power forwards Luis Scola and Carl Landry arrived to bolster the Houston frontcourt. Scola had finished third in the Rookie of the Year voting that season. After some early-season struggles, the Rockets began to win a few games in a row. Then, they did not stop winning. They won 12 games in a row, but then Yao Ming was suddenly declared out for the season with another knee injury. However, Dikembe Mutombo filled in admirably and McGrady led the way.

McGrady would score 30 points in his first game that season in a win against Kobe and the Lakers. In his next game, Tracy exploded for 47 points in a win in Utah. He made 17 out of 27 field goals in that game as well as 11 of 14 free throws. In a loss to Memphis on November 13, 2007, he would go for at least 40 points again as he netted 41 on 16 out of 28 shooting in just over 36 minutes.

On December 1st, Tracy McGrady scored 40 points in a loss to the Sacramento Kings. He made five three-pointers in that game. In his next game, he had his first triple-double of the season, recording 17 points, 10 rebounds, and 12 rebounds in a win against the Grizzlies. Despite a hot start on a personal level, T-Mac would eventually slow down as the season went on. We may be able to attribute some of that to his injuries, but it was primarily because of how well he played team basketball from then on. The Rockets were winning games while McGrady focused on getting other players involved.

The Houston Rockets would win 22 games in a row, which was, at the time, the second-longest winning streak in NBA history. McGrady was discussed once again as a possible contender for league MVP because of how well he orchestrated the Rockets' run without their 7'6" superstar center. T-Mac would only have four games of scoring at least 30 points in that historic winning streak.

He had 33 points and 11 rebounds in a win against Milwaukee on February 2, 2008. McGrady would then score 34 points against the Hornets 20 days later. Against the same team on March 8th, he had 41 points and 9 assists. In the Rockets' 21st consecutive win, Tracy had 30 points against Charlotte. Despite the historic winning streak and playing considerably well in that span of games, Tracy McGrady would not be chosen as an All-Star, particularly because young guards were quickly rising in the Western Conference.

On top of that, McGrady was already showing signs of deterioration because he was no longer the same player that he used to be. He was still 6'8" and equipped with scoring moves that even Bryant once feared. But he no longer had the same kind of lift that he used to have when it came to his jump shot and his ability to attack the basket. He was still a star-level player, but no longer the same athlete that had blown the minds of coaches, players, and fans alike.

For the season, Tracy McGrady averaged 21.6 points, 5.1 rebounds, and 5.9 assists. It would appear that his myriad of injuries were slowing him down, as he shot merely 41.9% from the floor and 29.2% from beyond the arc. For the first time since 2001, T-Mac was not the best scorer on the team; Yao edged him out by a slim margin in that department. Nevertheless, McGrady was still one of the best shooting guards in the league. He was named to the All-NBA third team particularly because he led the Rockets to a 22-game winning streak. The Houston Rockets finished the season with a record of 55 wins against 27 losses. The Rockets came into the playoffs with the fifth seed in the crowded Western Conference.

The Houston Rockets would once again face the Utah Jazz in the first round of the postseason. Though they had homecourt advantage, the Rockets would lose two straight games on their own floor to open the series. Despite the losses, T-Mac played the role of an all-around superstar as expected, as he rebounded and assisted well in both games. In Game 1, he had 20 points on 7 out of 21 shooting while also gathering 6 boards and 7 dimes. In Game 2, he nearly had a triple-double as he scored 23 points, 13 rebounds, and 9 assists. However, he shot 9 out of 22 from the field in that game, and his team would go down 0-2.

The Rockets would not fall into a 0-3 deficit, however, as they fought back to narrowly win Game 3 by two points. In Game 4, T-Mac had 23 points, 10 rebounds, and 8 assists, but the Jazz took that one by 4. McGrady next led his team to a big win in Game 5 as they extended the series to at least one more game. T-Mac had 29 points in that match.

However, the one-man show proved to be too difficult for Tracy. He was playing without Rafer Alston and Yao Ming, and that meant that he had to facilitate and rebound while handling the bulk of the scoring duties as well. In Game 6, T-Mac had 40 points, 10 rebounds, and 5 assists. Despite his best efforts, Utah won that game by 22. It was another first-round exit for Tracy McGrady and his team.

## The Beginning of the End

Despite the two bitter defeats to Utah, the Rockets had plenty to look forward to. Over the offseason, they acquired star defensive small forward Ron Artest from the Sacramento Kings. Also, Yao Ming was coming back into the season healthy. He would play 77 games in the regular season as his health was finally cooperating with him. It was clear that if the three players could remain healthy, Houston would be one of the most dangerous teams in the NBA.

But, after so many years of carrying mediocre teams to the playoffs and regular season wins, McGrady's body finally gave up on him. In May 2008, Tracy underwent knee and shoulder surgery, but it did nothing to alleviate his left knee pain.

While Tracy still had his moments here and there, such as a vicious dunk on Chicago Bulls forward Tyrus Thomas, his athleticism was mostly gone. Plus, he did not get along well with the team, and Ron

Artest (aka Metta World Peace) in particular. In a controversial game in January 2009 against Toronto, McGrady spent much of the game lingering around the half-court line and appeared to be completely ineffectual as the Rockets essentially played four on five.

Despite those moments, Tracy still had some great games in between mediocre and just plain bad ones. On November 6, 2008, he had his first and only 30-point game of the season when he scored 30 points and had 7 rebounds and 8 assists in a loss to Portland. He would have his first triple-double of the season on December 16th as he recorded 20 points, 14 rebounds, and 10 dimes in a win versus the Denver Nuggets. However, McGrady would never again have the same spectacular moments he'd had in Orlando or during his early years in Houston.

As had happened in Toronto and Orlando, relations between McGrady and Houston deteriorated. The Rockets began talking with other teams about trading him, such as to the New Jersey Nets in exchange for his cousin Vince. However, on February 18, 2009, and before a trade could materialize, McGrady underwent micro-fracture surgery on his troublesome left knee. It would keep him out for the rest of the regular season. McGrady averaged 15.6 points, 4.4 rebounds, and 5 assists in only 35 games that season. He shot a dismal 48.8% from the floor.

The Houston Rockets had to rely on Yao, Scola, Battier, and Artest, who would play shooting guard. Aaron Brooks also did well as a point guard from the bench. They went on to win 52 games and were the fifth seed once again. Without McGrady, the Rockets defeated the Portland Trail Blazers in the first round before losing to the Los Angeles Lakers. Technically, McGrady had finally passed the first round—but it was a meaningless statistic since he was wearing street clothes. He could not even play a single game in the playoffs as the Rockets won a first-round series for the first time since acquiring McGrady in 2004.

Houston made it as deep as the second round. So, in a sense, the Rockets had the ability to get past the first round. Unfortunately for McGrady, he was not around to play because of his injury. And that meant that he was still unable to see a single second of play in the second round of the playoffs throughout his entire career, despite the fact that he had made the playoffs multiple times at that point.

There was no longer denying that T-Mac was no longer the transcendental star that he used to be. It was clear that he could no longer lead a team or even stay healthy long enough to contribute on a consistent level. The former two-time scoring champion had now become a shell of his former self and was no longer going to affect a team's chances of making a deep playoff run. And that meant that his days in Houston were now running out.

During the 2009-10 season, McGrady once again became the subject of trade talks. He was on the last year of his superstar deal and was earning $23 million that season. Meanwhile, teams across the league that season were clearing cap space in preparation for pursuing LeBron James in the 2010 free agency period. If a team could unload a salary past 2010 in exchange for McGrady's expiring contract, it might improve their chances of getting LeBron or other great free-agent prospects such as Dwyane Wade and Chris Bosh.

McGrady played a few games as a bench player for the Rockets, but otherwise spent the season wearing suits instead of jerseys. He would only play a total of six games for the Rockets the whole season. He made his season debut on December 15, 2009, against the Denver Nuggets. Houston would win that game, but Tracy was limited to 3 points. He would play five more games for the Rockets before getting shut down late in December. He would only score a total of 19 points in about 7 minutes per game for Houston that season. Finally, on February 18, 2010, the long-awaited trade happened and Tracy McGrady was traded to the New York Knicks. He averaged merely 3.2 points in 7.7 minutes in his final six games in Houston.

At first, it seemed that the rumors of McGrady's downfall were greatly exaggerated. In his first game with the Knicks against the Oklahoma City Thunder, McGrady scored 26 points and had 5 assists in a narrow loss. He was 10 out of 17 from the field in that game. However, as the season progressed, it appeared that while McGrady could play like he used to in spurts, he could no longer do it over the grind of an entire NBA season. Nevertheless, he still had excellent moments with the Knicks.

In a win against the Washington Wizards, T-Mac had 23 points on 8 out of 17 shooting from the field in 25 minutes on February 26th. He then had 21 points, 7 rebounds, and 8 dimes in a blowout win against the Detroit Pistons on March 3rd. However, he would figure in double-digit scoring only seven more times in the next 17 games, as it appeared that the wear and tear of injuries had finally caught up with him. In his final five games of the season, he scored just 19 total points.

Tracy McGrady averaged a total of 8.2 points, 3.1 rebounds, and 3.3 assists in 22.4 minutes in the 30 games he played that season. He shot 38.7% from the floor. With the Knicks specifically, he averaged 9.4 points, 3.7 rebounds, and 3.9 assists in the 24 games he played. It appeared that McGrady's years as a productive player were all but done. The Knicks would miss the postseason with a poor record that season.

The downfall of one of the greatest wing players the early 2000s had ever seen was quick yet steady and methodical in its approach. And age was not the main factor in T-Mac's decline, because there were other superstars who were older and still playing at the highest level possible. For instance, his old rival and friend Kobe Bryant was still competing for championships while putting up elite numbers on the offensive end, despite the fact that he was already in his 30s.

There were numerous factors that led to T-Mac's downfall as a former superstar with transcendent abilities. The first culprit was his nagging back problem that started to plague him during the earlier part of his final year with the Orlando Magic. No one could blame him for having back problems because he was a lone star who had to carry a band of misfits to the playoffs throughout his four-year run with Orlando. Frankly, anyone who had to carry a team riddled with players who were basically nonfactors like that would likely have back problems! And, of course, McGrady was the top target of opposing defenses, and his body suffered a lot of bumps and bruises from defenders that could not stop him.

Those who have never experienced back problems would not understand this, but everything starts from the back. A person's back muscles are essential to athletic movements because these muscles are core muscles that help stabilize an athlete's movements. The core also assists in the many different explosive and athletic movements that a basketball player does, including jumping. In relation to that, McGrady's unstoppable jump shot, which was basically unguardable because of how high he jumped off the floor when shooting, was affected by his back problems. Thus, it goes without saying that he could no longer explode to the basket the same way as well.

When the back is having problems, all the other muscles that aid in a player's movements have to exert more effort. So, because of that, the wear and tear on the other muscles and joints tends to increase, thereby speeding up the deterioration of a player's athletic prowess. That was what happened to Tracy McGrady when he had to carry a team on his back during his prime years in Orlando.

Of course, McGrady was not without blame as well. The thing about him was that he was always far more talented than most of his peers in the NBA. He stood at least 6'8", could run the floor like a gazelle, had one of the quickest and widest first steps in the history of the league, and could shoot jumpers at a height that made him look like he was going for a dunk. On top of that, he had the handles of a true guard. This was why there were a lot of people who claimed that McGrady, at his peak, was a better player than Kobe Bryant. He had all the talent in the world and was banking almost entirely on his talent to succeed.

But because he was far more talented than his peers, it can be argued that he did not work as hard as they did. There was a point in his life wherein he was seemingly contented with relying on his talents rather than bothering to work harder on the other aspects of his game. He even admitted that he did not practice hard enough during his playing years.

"I just wasn't a great practice player,' McGrady said. 'I just wasn't. I wasn't. I just think I could cruise through practice and still be effective. Some guys have to really go all out to really have an impact on practice. My ability was just I had God-given talent to where I could just cruise through practice and still be an effective practice player ... I was inconsistent. Some days, I have really good practice days where I just go hard and a lot of days where like, 'Uh,' and I just go through the motions. But I work hard. But I'm just not the best practice player."[xiv]

His coach in Houston, Jeff Van Gundy, was even critical of his work ethic as he once said that McGrady was simply so talented that he felt like he was relying on his talents alone. So, one can theorize that, while his health affected his ability to play at a high level, working harder might have allowed him to keep his body in better shape or allow him to develop fundamental skills that did not require his athleticism. Relying more on fundamentals was a shift that many great players make as they age, but one that McGrady never endeavored to take.

One case in point was Kobe Bryant, who had more mileage on his body than McGrady because he played more times in the playoffs and was able to have deep playoff runs on his way to a total of seven finals appearances for the Los Angeles Lakers. Kobe's athleticism had deteriorated due to age, wear, and tear, but he understood well enough that he needed to work on his fundamentals to stay effective, and he did.

So, while the version of Kobe Bryant that won three straight championships from 2000 to 2002 was an athletic beast, the older version that won two straight championships in 2009 and 2010 was more of a fundamentally sound player who relied on footwork and post moves to get his shots off. Kobe worked hard on honing his jump shot without having to rely on his ability to jump high. As such, Bryant could score 20 or more points deep into his 30s even though he had already suffered numerous injuries throughout his career.

A more recent example of this shift in playing style would be LeBron James, who worked hard on his body and conditioning to make sure that he could play at an elite level during his late 30s. He may have worked hard on his fundamentals, but LeBron's bread and butter was his body, which allowed him to dominate his way to the all-time career scoring leadership. And James' work ethic during the offseason was legendary because he always made sure to spend time and money to stay as strong and conditioned as possible.

Even McGrady's cousin, Vince Carter, played until he was 43 years old because he took care of his body. Of course, Carter fell from his All-Star level right around the same time as T-Mac did. But he augmented his deteriorating athleticism with his jump shot and by taking care of his body deep into his 30s.

In McGrady's case, he had all the talent and resources in the world, but he just did not work and practice as hard as the other superstars. The point to be made here is that a true all-time great needs to have a good combination of work ethic and talent, because talent alone will never suffice. Meanwhile, working hard will only get a player so far if he does not have the talent necessary to become great in the first place.

There is no question that T-Mac had the talent of an all-time great— but he also suffered the worst possible luck when he landed on subpar teams. And to compound that issue, he did not try to work harder to neutralize that bad luck, or to adjust his playing style when it became clear that the grind of carrying those subpar teams was taking its toll and whittling away at his prime playing years.

With all that said, McGrady's downfall was brought about by multiple factors. Some of those factors were within his control, while others were not. And at that point in his career, it was already too late to look back at what he could have done because he was already entering the final stages of what was once an impressive career.

# End Days of a Once-Great Superstar, Retirement

For the 2010-11 season, Tracy McGrady found himself signing with the Detroit Pistons to a one-year deal worth the veteran's minimum. It was more of the same for McGrady in Detroit, as he was playing on a team with washed-up veterans Tayshaun Prince, Richard Hamilton, Ben Wallace, and Ben Gordon. The Pistons would not be competitive that season. Still, Tracy was able to show flashes of his former superstar self.

Through his first 20 games of the season, T-Mac figured in double-digit scoring only twice. He also had five games of scoring zero points during that span. His best output was a 13-point game when he shot 6 out of 10 from the field in a loss to the Knicks on November 28, 2010. On December 14th, McGrady seemed to have found a small spark in himself as he scored 16 points on 5 out of 9 shooting from the floor and 4 out of 6 from the three-point line in a 23-point win versus the Atlanta Hawks. He then had 17 points, 7 rebounds, and 7 assists in 24 minutes as the Pistons beat Toronto by 22 points on December 22nd.

On December 29th, T-Mac turned the hands of time back as he scored 21 points and grabbed 8 boards in a win against the Celtics. On January 3, 2011, he had his first double-double game with 11 points and 11 rebounds in a loss to the Jazz. Eleven days later, he had 22 points in 35 minutes as the Pistons won a game in Toronto. On January 24th, he had 20 points in a seven-point win against the Orlando Magic, the team he had played his best for back in his heyday.

On January 28th, T-Mac flirted with a triple-double as he finished a loss to the Miami Heat with 14 points, 8 rebounds, and 10 assists. On February 5th, he had 20 points for the final time that season as he led an 11-point win versus the Milwaukee Bucks. That was the end game of a seven-game streak of scoring in double digits for Tracy McGrady.

On February 23, 2011, he had his final double-double game with 16 points and 12 dimes in a loss to the Indiana Pacers. That was the fifth game of six straight outings of scoring at least 10 points. For the season, Tracy McGrady averaged 8 points, 3.5 rebounds, and 3.5 assists in 23.4 minutes of action. He played a total of 72 games and started in 39 of those. The Pistons did not qualify for the playoffs as they won merely 30 games.

McGrady then signed with the Atlanta Hawks for one year as the 2011-12 season unfolded. He was signed on to back Joe Johnson at the wing position. As the NBA was shortened with a lockout that season, Tracy had a lot of time to rest as the season started late in December. However, the compressed 66-game schedule would also be a bad thing for T-Mac as his rest time in between games was shortened.

T-Mac made his season debut on December 27, 2011, against the New Jersey Nets. The Hawks won that one by 36 big points. McGrady contributed with 12 points in that game. He then scored 11 as Atlanta won the next game by 18. On January 2, 2012, Tracy scored 16 points on 5 out of 8 shooting from the field versus the Miami Heat. He also had seven rebounds and four assists in 25 minutes of action in that win against a powerhouse team.

On January 31st, he scored 15 points in a 23-point win against the Toronto Raptors. From that point on, T-Mac would only score in double digits once until April. It appeared that his body could no longer handle the grind of the NBA. It also seemed like his days in the big leagues were now numbered. From April 13th to the 18th, T-Mac had a good three-game stretch. He produced consecutive games of scoring 11 points in two blowout wins versus the Orlando Magic and the Toronto Raptors, the two teams he first played for in his younger days. He then had 17 in the final game of that stretch as he torched another team he had played for, the Detroit Pistons.

In the 2011-12 season, Tracy McGrady averaged 5.3 points, 3 rebounds, and 2.1 assists in 16 minutes of action. He shot 43.7% from the floor and 45.5% from downtown in that season. T-Mac played 52 games in what would appear to be his final full regular season run in the NBA. The Hawks qualified for the playoffs as the fifth seed in the Eastern Conference as they won 40 out of 66 total games that season.

The Hawks faced the Boston Celtics in the first round of the playoffs. Though Atlanta won Game 1, they lost the next three. T-Mac combined for just 7 points in the first two games before going for 12 in Game 3. In a Game 5 victory, he didn't even contribute a single point to the cause. The Hawks would bow out of the postseason with a loss in Game 6. Tracy scored 4 points in what seemed to be the final playoff game he would play in his career.

Since no NBA team would sign Tracy McGrady entering the 2012-13 season, he decided to try his hand overseas. T-Mac signed with the Qingdao Double Star Eagles of the Chinese Basketball Association. For that single season, he somehow looked like the Tracy McGrady of old. In China, he averaged 25 points, 7.2 rebounds, 5.1 assists, and 1.6 steals. McGrady shot 49.6% from the field in that season and 33.3% from beyond the three-point line. He was the Eagles' second-leading scorer behind big man Robert Daniels. Despite his stellar numbers, Qingdao finished last place in the CBA. However, McGrady wasn't quite done as he would find himself back in the NBA for one last time.

In the final days of the 2012-13 season, the San Antonio Spurs suddenly signed McGrady. They had released swingman Stephen Jackson after he had thrown a temper tantrum and were looking for someone to take Jackson's roster spot. The Spurs were the second-seeded team in the West that season. They had legitimate title aspirations with or without Tracy McGrady.

In the first round of the playoffs, the Spurs swept the Los Angeles Lakers in four games. At the end of Game 4, as San Antonio blew out the Lakers, Coach Gregg Popovich put McGrady on the court. For the first time in his career, McGrady had officially played on a team that had gotten past the first round, although he did not score in that game.

The Spurs then went on to beat the Golden State Warriors in six Games in the second round. McGrady showed up for two games in that series. He played for a total of barely 5 minutes in two games versus the Warriors. Again, he did not score a single point in his limited time on the floor. He then did not score a single point in the one game he appeared in during the four-game sweep of the Memphis Grizzlies in the Western Conference Finals.

In the NBA Finals, the Spurs were up 3-2 heading into Game 6 against the Miami Heat. In the previous five games, Tracy played a total of about 14 minutes. He did not score in those games. Despite that, he was still able to say that he had appeared and played in the NBA Finals. Not a lot of players get to say that. With the Spurs up by 5 points in the final 30 seconds or so of Game 6, McGrady could be seen hooking arms with his teammates on the bench in anticipation of a possible NBA ring. However, the Miami Heat made a miraculous run to force overtime and win Game 6. The Heat would go on to win Game 7 and the NBA championship.

In his final moments as an NBA player, Tracy McGrady was denied of an NBA championship. On August 26, 2013, McGrady officially retired from the NBA game at the age of 34 years old.

## Getting Immortalized in the Hall of Fame

There are a lot of things that people could—and *did*—say about Tracy McGrady. Some said that he was all talent but no hard work. Then, there are those who said that he simply had the worst possible luck. But while there are some truths behind all of those words, what became the ultimate truth was that he was inducted into the Hall of Fame as a part of the Class of 2017.

Of course, some critics did not believe that he was worthy of entering the Hall of Fame. McGrady himself almost did not even believe that he was worthy of being recognized as one of the most influential basketball players in his era. After all, he understood that he did not have the best accomplishments in his career because he never won an MVP and was never able to achieve a championship ring. Despite that, he found the strength to admit that he had what it took to become immortalized as a Hall-of-Fame player.

"It's way too easy to focus on what you don't have than what you didn't accomplish, and I'm grateful for those people that saw in me, believed in me, when, just maybe, when I always didn't believe in myself," McGrady said in his Hall-of-Fame induction speech. "People who actually saw the man and not just the athlete."[xv]

But he went on to say that he learned in the 15 years of his basketball career that he persevered and believed in himself well enough to push himself through all the challenges that he had to go through in his entire NBA run. And while he failed to win a championship or any other individual award that held the same weight, he ultimately realized that he gave himself a chance, which was more than enough for him to get recognized as a true trail-blazing star in the history of the league.

# Chapter 4: Personal Life

Tracy McGrady married his longtime love, CleRenda Harris, in 2006, after they had already been a couple for 10 years. They have three children—two boys, Laymen and Layden, and a girl, Layla. Fun fact: Laymen, their first son, was born during a Rockets home game in December 2005, and Tracy had to leave the game at halftime to attend the birth!

Despite his prodigal basketball ability, McGrady has had time to pursue interests other than basketball. As a major superstar in his prime, McGrady was sponsored by Adidas and signed a lifetime contract with the shoe company. The Adidas T-Mac shoe line came out in 2002, and constant renovations over the next six years (along with McGrady's rise to stardom) kept the sneakers in the spotlight as some of the best basketball shoes in the country. A young LeBron James playing basketball in Akron, Ohio, was reportedly a huge fan! Sadly, the T-Mac line hasn't existed since 2008, as production was discontinued around the time that Tracy's reign as a superstar came to an end. Those sneakers are now prized collectibles, and still highly sought after by fans.

After his retirement, one of McGrady's biggest goals was to return to baseball, the sport that he had loved so much as a little boy. Tracy decided to play as a pitcher and worked with legendary pitcher-turned-coach Roger Clemens to improve for about four months. He then signed with the Sugar Land Skeeters in the Atlantic League, a baseball league independent of the MLB which is somewhere in between the AA and AAA leagues. McGrady played just 6-2/3 innings over four games. He was unimpressive and finished with a 6.75 ERA, but in his final game at the Atlantic League's All-Star Game, he finally struck out an opposing batter. After the game, McGrady duly announced his retirement and thanked the Atlantic League for giving him the chance to play baseball once again.

McGrady has also made time to give back to the less fortunate. He and his wife CleRenda are both generous philanthropists and are very passionate about their many charitable endeavors. While most NBA stars do some form of charity work here and there, Tracy went above and beyond with his efforts in the Darfur region of Sudan. During the mid-2000s, Darfur was undergoing severe chaos due to a civil war involving ethnic conflicts. Tracy decided to visit the region in 2007 to see the situation for himself. He donated money to improve the lives of the children there, and later authored a documentary about his visit as well as the plight of the Darfur refugees. McGrady called it *3 Points* after the three desires of "peace, protection, and punishment." In September 2009, the documentary was released on Hulu to great acclaim. He even changed his jersey number from 1 to 3 to promote his documentary and kept the number throughout his 2009-10 NBA season.

Tracy has dabbled in real estate, done some investing, and has worked as a basketball analyst for ESPN as well. He remains an outspoken presence on social media, and of course, basketball is still a big part of his life. In 2022, Tracy founded the Ones Basketball League (aka the OBL), a one-on-one basketball league that showcases some of the most impressive talent that can be found outside of the NBA. It is a fitting, heartfelt tribute to the street game that paved his own way to the NBA, and Tracy hopes that it can do the same for others.

"To me, there has always been some untapped talent outside the NBA, and even leagues outside the U.S.," Tracy commented about the OBL. "I thought creating a platform and a league could showcase some of that talent."

# Chapter 5: Impact on Basketball

To talk about Tracy McGrady's impact on the NBA is to speak of the importance of things that cannot be measured by statistics. One of the main criticisms of McGrady is that, while he was an incredibly talented basketball player, he lacked the little things that distinguished the greatest players from the merely excellent. How good of a leader was McGrady on and off the court? Did he set an example for the rest of his lesser teammates? Was he willing to take over down the stretch?

McGrady was so talented and succeeded so quickly that some people wondered whether he truly cared about basketball. And McGrady's perennially disinterested expression and sleepy eyes did not help to convince his critics that he wanted to win above all else. (Speaking of *sleepy*, McGrady was notorious for sleeping long hours and napping frequently throughout his career. He once scored 41 points in a game despite the fact that he had been sound asleep until just before tip-off!) Given Orlando's and later Houston's inability to get past the first round of the playoffs when he was a star, how could it be said that McGrady was a winner?

So, what were McGrady's intangibles like, and how important are these little things?

There is no denying that traits like leadership and hard work have some importance in basketball. As much as people want to talk about "The Popovich system" in the aftermath of San Antonio's dominant performance in the 2014 Finals, Popovich is the first to admit that the system still revolved around Tim Duncan, who was well known for his hard work and commitment to the team.

However, much of the discussion about intangibles becomes a quid pro quo argument. Player X won, therefore he had good intangibles. Player Y lost, therefore he had bad intangibles. Perhaps the best example of this style of "discussion" is LeBron James.

When LeBron left for Miami, a common criticism was that he lacked these intangibles and thus had to depend on Dwyane Wade. But after LeBron won two championships as the undisputed best player on the Miami Heat, those criticisms have vanished. While there is room for the discussion of intangibles as part of a player's legacy, we must be careful not to overstate it too much. It is entirely possible for a player to have good intangibles but still not have player success. Kevin Garnett is a perfect example of this phenomenon.

Now, what about Tracy McGrady? It is true that despite—or perhaps because of—his prodigal gifts, McGrady was not a natural leader. At times, he would let his emotions get the better of his reason. With the Magic, he openly criticized the front offices for some of their trades. During a FIBA game in 2003, he got into a major fight with the Puerto Rico team. On February 21, 2004, an angry T-Mac punted the basketball into the stands—*twice*!

When Tracy was with the Rockets, Coach Jeff Van Gundy led the team emotionally. When the Rockets replaced Van Gundy with Rick

Adelman, Adelman tried to shift McGrady into more of a leadership role. But McGrady demurred, and the leadership role for that team fell not to T-Mac or even to Yao but to role players Shane Battier, Dikembe Mutombo, and Chuck Hayes.

But if the role players on the Rockets were the leaders, then how important was leadership? It is not like McGrady struggled in his first-round defeats. McGrady *did* raise his game in the playoffs. While he averaged 19.6 points over his entire regular season career, he averaged 22 points in the playoffs. He had big games in Game 7 of the 2007 Playoffs and Game 6 of the 2008 Playoffs, but the Houston Rockets still lost. While McGrady may have never been a vocal or inspiring leader, to claim that his lack of playoff success is somehow due to his lack of leadership is wrong.

Tracy may not have been like Michael Jordan or Kobe Bryant, both of whom led their teams by pushing them to their limits in games and practices. He may not have been like Kevin Garnett, who showed all of his emotions as a leader on the floor. He may not have been like LeBron James, who leads all of his teams by befriending everyone and making them look good on the floor. He may not be like Tim Duncan, who was an extension of Popovich on the floor. However, McGrady did his best as a leader by playing hard every single game. But that was never enough for a superstar like him.

At the end of the day, few superstars in league history had less help in the league than Tracy McGrady. Had McGrady chosen not to leave the Raptors (a decision he has admitted he regrets), how would he be remembered differently? What if Grant Hill or Yao Ming had not suffered injury issues, or if the Rockets or Magic had given him a decent supporting team?

And that is what we should remember McGrady for. Perhaps McGrady could have worked harder, or could have been a better leader. Still, the reality is that the defining feature of his career was the lack of help and poor supporting team members which prevented him from being remembered as fondly as he should have.

Nevertheless, true fans of the game will always remember him fondly enough because he left a lasting impression on the memories of those who followed his entire career. The game was always about putting the ball through the basket, and no one did it like Tracy McGrady, who was a trailblazer at his position because no one was quite like him before he broke out and became one of the best players in the league during his peak.

The guy was 6'8" and probably even an inch taller than that during his best years in the league. However, he played like a true shooting guard who had all the tools in the bag. No one could guard him back then because he had the height of a power forward and the lift of a small forward. On top of that, his wingspan and shooting abilities were transcendental. And it was his overall talent that made him a joy to watch for a lot of NBA fans.

So, while he may not have had the greatest career, his impact was lasting because he was the first player that most kids who grew up in the 2000s would remember if they imagined a shooting guard other than Kobe Bryant. He had all the tools of an all-time great. And the only thing that we could have wished was that he was just as lucky as he was talented.

# Chapter 6: Legacy

McGrady's legacy in the NBA is difficult to assess. At the height of his popularity, he was viewed as a superstar on the same level as Kobe Bryant and Tim Duncan. There was nothing McGrady could not do. He was an excellent rebounder and passer for a tall shooting guard, he could defend, drive to the rim, and score from absolutely anywhere. He was the scoring champion twice and made the All-NBA and All-Star Teams seven times.

In his prime, he could even say that he was the best shooting guard the NBA has seen since Michael Jordan. Yes, McGrady was even better than Kobe Bryant, Allen Iverson, and Vince Carter when he was in peak form. You could even argue that Tracy was the best individual player in his heyday. That was how good he was. But, somehow, his talent was never enough to solidify an already established resume.

Despite McGrady's impressive resume, his lack of playoff success sticks out like a sore thumb. In his years as a star, Tracy never made it past the first round. In 2003, his Orlando Magic led the top-seeded Detroit Pistons 3 games to 1. In 2005, the Houston Rockets won the first two games of the series at Dallas. In 2007, the Rockets also won their first two games against Utah. But in every single situation, the opposing team rallied and eventually won the series, in spite of strong performances from McGrady. Unlike other superstars, McGrady didn't choke in those playoff series. He played his heart out every single game. However, he could never make his role players play as hard as he did. And the only factor we could blame was the makeup of his team because the Magic squads that he led were downright mediocre or even worse.

We have already discussed above how McGrady's lack of playoff success actually cannot be tied to him. However, had he worked harder to take care of his body, perhaps he could have avoided the injury problems which ended his career prematurely. Or perhaps the strain of carrying inferior franchises proved to be too much for him, but it is impossible to say with any certainty either way.

The reality is that, while we do not like to acknowledge it, winning a championship frequently carries with it a degree of luck. Would Kobe Bryant have prevailed in 2009 had it not been for the injuries of Yao Ming and Kevin Garnett? That was a legitimate question given how the Rockets pushed the Lakers to the limit in that series.

Would LeBron James have prevailed in 2013 if Ray Allen had not hit the greatest tying shot in the history of the NBA? McGrady could have won a title had Allen not hit that clutch shot.

Would Tim Duncan have prevailed in 2007 if the Golden State Warriors had not shockingly upset the No. 1 seed Dallas Mavericks in the first round? It is impossible to know. But while we may talk confidently about "winners" and "losers" in basketball, if there are those who are luckier than most and blessed with good teammates, then it must stand that there are those who are unluckier. And Tracy McGrady was definitely among the latter.

His peers understand this. When TV talk show host Jimmy Kimmel asked Kobe in 2013, "Who was the toughest guy you played against?" Kobe's answer was McGrady. Yes, he answered Tracy McGrady! In his prime years, McGrady was arguably better than Kobe was. He had the size and the skills to outmatch anybody at his position. Though Kobe would turn out to be the better player at an all-time rate because of his longevity and his championships, there can be no argument that he and T-Mac were on par back in the day. Magic Johnson called McGrady one of the greatest scorers in history. And McGrady's thin, lanky frame inspired future similar wings like Kevin Durant, Paul George, and Jayson Tatum on their own paths to NBA stardom.

Today, you see long and tall guys like Durant and George dominating the offensive end because of how they pose matchup problems for other teams. Durant stands nearly 7 feet tall and has the ball-handling abilities of a point guard and the shooting skills of an off guard much like McGrady in his prime years.

Durant has dominated the NBA with his scoring abilities as he could shoot over smaller defenders and outrun guys his size. In George's case, he stands nearly 6'9" and has long arms. Paul George does most of his damage on the defensive end, unlike Tracy. However, when he gets it going on offense, he's nearly as unstoppable as McGrady was because of how much taller and more athletic he is than the other guys at his position. If you look at the prototype for those two players, the one player you would immediately think of is Tracy McGrady. And then there is Jayson Tatum, who patterned his game after Kobe but was always more like Tracy McGrady because of his lanky 6'8" frame.

McGrady was the first of his kind in the sense that there was no other player with his set of skills at his height. George Gervin was great at 6'7" but was not the same shooter that T-Mac was. Julius "Dr. J" Erving was the same athlete as McGrady but lacked the offensive firepower that T-Mac had from the perimeter. Michael Jordan and Kobe Bryant were similar to him. But McGrady, at nearly 6'9", was taller than those players. In that regard, he was the first of his kind as he led the way for tall and talented wings to dominate the league with the shooting of an off-guard, the athleticism of a small forward, and the handles of a point guard.

If we were to put T-Mac in the current generation, he would have easily averaged over 30 points per game due to the spacing and pacing that the modern-day NBA has. As such, he would have easily dominated the league today as well because he had all of the tools that most of the superstar wings of today's generation also have.

As good as Tracy McGrady was in his prime, he still could not escape criticism. McGrady's injuries had slowed him down as early as 29 years old. At that age, Michael Jordan was still winning titles and scoring championships. Kobe Bryant was putting up 60 points on the board. Vince Carter and Clyde Drexler were still dunking on their opponents. But what about McGrady?

McGrady could not be blamed for the injuries he suffered. However, he is not the only wing player who suffered severe injuries. Both Jordan and Bryant have had a myriad of injuries throughout their legendary careers. However, as both those guys lost their athleticism and their explosiveness due to age and injuries, they were still able to dominate.

How did they do that? They fueled themselves with their desire to compete and to be the best to work harder and harder. Mike and Kobe honed their midrange game to be virtually un-guardable. They worked on their footwork and moves at the low post to bully their opponents into submission. That's how they were able to play at superstar levels as they aged into their deep 30s. At the age of 34, T-Mac could not even score a single point in the playoffs when he played for the Spurs.

One can also say that Tracy McGrady's refusal to change his style of play has cost him several productive years in the NBA. Going back to Jordan and Bryant, both were athletic beasts in their younger years but transitioned into perimeter and post scorers as they aged. Even Vince Carter, Ray Allen, and Clyde Drexler made the transition. Carter played up to his 40s because he improved his three-point shot. Ray Allen played well as he neared his 40s because he shot the three-pointer very well despite being an all-around scorer in his younger years. Drexler played at a star level until the day he retired because he honed his jump shot.

Meanwhile, Tracy McGrady almost always relied on his natural talent and athleticism to score even when he couldn't rely on his body anymore because of his injuries. Had he at least had half the work ethic of Michael and Kobe or the shooting of a Ray Allen, Tracy McGrady could have still been playing great despite his age and his infirmities.

Despite some setbacks and criticisms in his career, there is no argument that Tracy McGrady's best years came when he was the superstar of the Orlando Magic. He was in Orlando when he was named the Most Improved Player and was a member of the All-NBA first team twice and the All-NBA second team once. It was in Orlando where he had his first four All-Star seasons. It was in Orlando that Tracy McGrady was the best scorer the NBA had to offer for two consecutive seasons. But where does he belong in the annals of Orlando Magic history?

The Orlando Magic is one of the youngest teams in the NBA. They only started as a franchise back in 1989 when McGrady was a young boy living nearby. In the Magic's short history, they have produced household names such as Shaquille O'Neal, Penny Hardaway, and Dwight Howard. While there is no argument that Shaq is the best player in Magic history, T-Mac is not far behind him. With his long years and his success as a franchise player in Orlando, one can argue that Dwight Howard ranks higher than Tracy in Magic history. That may be true, but McGrady is still the best perimeter player the franchise has ever seen.

In only four seasons in Orlando, T-Mac scored 8,298 points, which ranks third in franchise history. That's more than what Penny scored with the Magic even though the latter played more years in Orlando. Tracy played the same number of seasons as Shaq did in Orlando, but he scored more points than the Big Diesel. And though Dwight Howard spent four more seasons with the Magic than McGrady, he only leads the latter by about 3,200 career points. That's how much of an amazing scorer Tracy was in his days in Orlando. He gave two scoring championships to Orlando and brought the excitement back to that part of Florida. Had the Magic given him the right supporting cast, McGrady would have stayed longer there and he might have even brought them more playoff glory than what he produced in his four seasons as a one-man show in Orlando.

On a regular season basis, T-Mac saw more success in Houston than any other team he's played for. He was teamed up with the 7'6" Chinese center Yao Ming. The two players formed matchup nightmares for their opponents as they were both taller and bigger than most of the players at their respective positions. They could have been a great inside-outside duo that would have rivaled historical duos of the same caliber such as Shaq and Kobe, and Wilt and Jerry. However, injuries got to both players as they were hindered from playing their best on the floor. They were never able to garner the postseason success everyone thought they could get. Nevertheless, T-Mac is still one of the best players in Houston Rockets history as he is third in points per game in franchise history with 22.7. He spent about four and a half seasons in Houston and was an All-Star in three of those years.

McGrady was an All-Star in Orlando four times. He then went to Houston to become a three-time All-Star as a Rocket. For seven wonderful years, Tracy McGrady was amongst the very best the NBA had to offer. He could even be arguably better than anyone the league had back in his prime years in Orlando. So, even if he never had the good luck or the health to be as good as he perhaps could have been, he should still be remembered as an all-time great.

In 2017, Tracy McGrady was given his rightful place in the annals of basketball history when he walked up to the podium in Springfield, Massachusetts, ready to deliver his speech during his induction into the Naismith Basketball Hall of Fame. He was, after all, one of the best shooting guards the NBA has ever seen in its long history. And those who know basketball will always fondly remember T-Mac for the transcendental star he truly was.

# Final Word/About the Author

I was born and raised in Norwalk, Connecticut. Growing up, I could often be found spending many nights watching basketball, soccer, and football matches with my father in the family living room. I love sports and everything that sports can embody. I believe that sports are one of the most genuine forms of competition, heart, and determination. I write my works to learn more about influential athletes in the hopes that from my writing, you the reader can walk away inspired to put in an equal if not greater amount of hard work and perseverance to pursue your goals. If you enjoyed *Tracy McGrady: The Inspiring Story of One of Basketball's Greatest Shooting Guards*, please leave a review! Also, you can read more of my works on *David Ortiz, Cody Bellinger, Alex Bregman, Francisco Lindor, Shohei Ohtani, Ronald Acuna Jr., Javier Baez, Jose Altuve, Christian Yelich, Max Scherzer, Mookie Betts, Pete Alonso, Clayton Kershaw, Mike Trout, Bryce Harper, Jackie Robinson, Justin Verlander, Derek Jeter, Ichiro Suzuki, Ken Griffey Jr., Babe Ruth, Aaron Judge, Novak Djokovic, Roger Federer, Rafael Nadal, Serena Williams, Naomi Osaka, Coco Gauff, Baker Mayfield, George Kittle, Matt Ryan, Matthew Stafford, Eli Manning, Khalil Mack, Davante Adams, Terry Bradshaw, Jimmy Garoppolo, Philip Rivers, Von Miller, Aaron Donald, Joey Bosa, Josh Allen, Mike Evans, Joe Burrow, Carson Wentz Adam Thielen, Stefon Diggs, Lamar Jackson, Dak Prescott, Patrick Mahomes, Odell Beckham Jr., J.J. Watt, Colin Kaepernick, Aaron Rodgers, Tom Brady, Russell Wilson, Peyton*

*Manning, Drew Brees, Calvin Johnson, Brett Favre, Rob Gronkowski, Andrew Luck, Richard Sherman, Bill Belichick, Candace Parker, Skylar Diggins-Smith, A'ja Wilson, Lisa Leslie, Sue Bird, Diana Taurasi, Julius Erving, Clyde Drexler, John Havlicek, Oscar Robertson, Ja Morant, Gary Payton, Khris Middleton, Michael Porter Jr., Julius Randle, Jrue Holiday, Domantas Sabonis, Mike Conley Jr., Jerry West, Dikembe Mutombo, Fred VanVleet, Jamal Murray, Zion Williamson, Brandon Ingram, Jaylen Brown, Charles Barkley, Trae Young, Andre Drummond, JJ Redick, DeMarcus Cousins, Wilt Chamberlain, Bradley Beal, Rudy Gobert, Aaron Gordon, Kristaps Porzingis, Nikola Vucevic, Andre Iguodala, Devin Booker, John Stockton, Jeremy Lin, Chris Paul, Pascal Siakam, Jayson Tatum, Gordon Hayward, Nikola Jokic, Bill Russell, Victor Oladipo, Luka Doncic, Ben Simmons, Shaquille O'Neal, Joel Embiid, Donovan Mitchell, Damian Lillard, Giannis Antetokounmpo, Chris Bosh, Kemba Walker, Isaiah Thomas, DeMar DeRozan, Amar'e Stoudemire, Al Horford, Yao Ming, Marc Gasol, Draymond Green, Kawhi Leonard, Dwyane Wade, Ray Allen, Pau Gasol, Dirk Nowitzki, Jimmy Butler, Paul Pierce, Manu Ginobili, Pete Maravich, Larry Bird, Kyle Lowry, Jason Kidd, David Robinson, LaMarcus Aldridge, Derrick Rose, Paul George, Kevin Garnett, Michael Jordan, LeBron James, Kyrie Irving, Klay Thompson, Stephen Curry, Kevin Durant, Russell Westbrook, Chris Paul, Blake Griffin, Kobe Bryant, Anthony Davis, Joakim Noah, Scottie Pippen, Carmelo Anthony, Kevin Love, Grant Hill, Vince Carter, Patrick Ewing, Karl Malone, Tony Parker, Allen*

116

*Iverson, Hakeem Olajuwon, Reggie Miller, Michael Carter-Williams, James Harden, John Wall, Tim Duncan, Steve Nash, Gregg Popovich, Pat Riley, John Wooden, Steve Kerr, Brad Stevens, Red Auerbach, Doc Rivers, Erik Spoelstra, Mike D'Antoni,* and *Phil Jackson* in the Kindle Store. If you love basketball, check out my website at claytongeoffreys.com to join my exclusive list where I let you know about my latest books and give you lots of goodies.

# Like what you read? Please leave a review!

I write because I love sharing the stories of influential athletes like Tracy McGrady with fantastic readers like you. My readers inspire me to write more so please do not hesitate to let me know what you thought by leaving a review! If you love books on life, basketball, or productivity, check out my website at claytongeoffreys.com to join my exclusive list where I let you know about my latest books. Aside from being the first to hear about my latest releases, you can also download a free copy of *33 Life Lessons: Success Principles, Career Advice & Habits of Successful People*. See you there!

*Clayton*

# References

[i] "Tracy McGrady Biography". JockBio. Web.

[ii] Crothers, Tim. "Onward Christian soldier". *Sports Illustrated*. 10 February 1997. Web.

[iii] Villanueva, Virgil. "Tracy McGrady on why he switched to basketball from baseball". *Basketball Network*. 15 September 2022. Web.

[iv] Rucket, Tyler. "Tracy McGrady uncovers why he chose to wear #1 on his jersey: "Penny became my idol… I saw myself in Penny"". *Sportskeeda*. 27 October 2022. Web.

[v] Fuoco, Roy. "McGrady recalls his basketball roots at Auburndale". *The Ledger*. 23 July 2017. Web.

[vi] Martinez, Johnnie. "I saw how those boys was living, I said, this is where I want to go to school" - Tracy McGrady reveals the NCAA college he would have considered going to". *Sportskeeda*. 8 November 2022. Web.

[vii] Merida, Kevin. "If the shoes fit". *The Washington Post*. 17 April 1998. Web.

[viii] Freeman, Eric. "Tracy McGrady thinks NBA players need two years of college". *Yahoo Sports*. 11 June 2013. Web.

[ix] "Shooting guards." *Ibiblio.org*. Web.

[x] Scott, Jelani. "Vince Carter, Tracy McGrady Share How They Discovered They Are Cousins". *Sports Illustrated*. 11 March 2023. Web.

[xi] Sheppard, Riley. "Magic Legend Tracy McGrady Reflects on Orlando Career: 'I Surprised Myself'". *Sports Illustrated*. 2 January 2023. Web.

[xii] Stein, Marc. "Vince, Tracy no longer a family feud". *ESPN*. 23 January 2001. Web.

[xiii] Silva, Orlando. "Kobe Bryant Revealed The Toughest Players He Had To Guard In The NBA". *Yard Barker*. 11 January 2023. Web.

[xiv] "Tracy McGrady Admits He Didn't Practice Hard". *Slam*. 16 March 2011. Web.

[xv] Tsuji, Alysha. "Tracy McGrady explains why he didn't believe he belonged in the Hall of Fame in speech". *For the Win*. 8 September

2017. Web.

Made in the USA
Coppell, TX
21 November 2024

40644611R00069